LEGALESE

THE WORDS
LAWYERS USE
AND
WHAT THEY MEAN

QUANTITY SALES

Most Dell books are available at special quantity discounts when purchased in bulk by corporations, organizations, and special-interest groups. Custom imprinting or excerpting can also be done to fit special needs. For details write: Dell Publishing, 666 Fifth Avenue, New York, NY 10103. Attn.: Special Sales Department.

INDIVIDUAL SALES

Are there any Dell books you want but cannot find in your local stores? If so, you can order them directly from us. You can get any Dell book in print. Simply include the book's title, author, and ISBN number if you have it, along with a check or money order (no cash can be accepted) for the full retail price plus $2.00 to cover shipping and handling. Mail to: Dell Readers Service, P.O. Box 5057, Des Plaines, IL 60017.

LEGALESE

THE WORDS
LAWYERS USE
AND
WHAT THEY MEAN

Miriam Kurtzig Freedman, J.D.

A LAUREL BOOK

Published by
Dell Publishing
a division of
Bantam Doubleday Dell
Publishing Group, Inc.
666 Fifth Avenue
New York, New York 10103

This book is not intended as a substitute for legal advice of an attorney. The reader should consult an attorney for matters relating to any particular legal issue.

ISBN: 0-440-20653-7

Printed in the United States of America
Published simultaneously in Canada
November 1990

10 9 8 7 6 5 4 3 2 1

Design: Stanley S. Drate/Folio Graphics Co. Inc.

OPM

To Dan, Julie, and Paul

ACKNOWLEDGMENTS

At first it was but an idea. Now it's a book! Along the way I had wonderful help and support. I wish to thank the following people for generously sharing their expertise and time in critiquing various sections of the book: Harold Brown, Paul Cirel, Alan Cohen, Harold Just, Patricia Nelson, Barbara Resnek, Lindsay Robertson, Robert Tuchman, Nikki Zapol, and Anna Zytkov; Susan Guth for research; Audrey Cayne for artwork in those early days; and all those family members and friends who tracked the progress of this book. Sometimes just to ask, "How's your book doing?" was enough! Thanks also to my colleagues at Stoneman, Chandler & Miller, and particularly Robert Fraser, for his invaluable upbeat support; my agent, Gail Ross, for her belief in the project all the way; and finally, my husband and children, to whom this book is dedicated with love.

CONTENTS

THE BASICS

Laws We Know Intuitively   3
Law and Equity   6
Criminal and Civil Laws: What Are the
   Differences?   9
Laws, Statutes, Regulations, and Canons   11
Who Is a Person?   16

CIVIL LAW AND LAWSUITS

Torts   27
Contracts (K's)   39
Marriage and Divorce: The Basics   48
Wills   54
Individual Income Taxes   60
Malpractice   68
The Amazing Life of a Check   71
Real Estate: The Law of Home Sweet Home   73
Landlord and Tenant Law   83
Remedies   87

KEY CONCEPTS IN CIVIL AND CRIMINAL LAW

Jurisdiction   95
Standard of Proof   101
Time and Its Legal Consequences   102
Full Faith and Credit   107
When What Is in Your Heart and Mind Does
    Matter   108
Defenses   112

CRIMINAL LAW

Felonies, Misdemeanors, and Violations   117
Larceny: In How Many Ways Can Someone
    Steal?   119
Homicide   122
Punishment   123

LEGAL PROCEDURES AND COURTS

Who's Who in the Courtroom   129
Documents   132
Basic Procedure in a Criminal Case   136
Basic Procedure in a Civil Case   142
Small Claims Court   148
When the Sheriff Is at the Door   151
Alternative Dispute Resolution, or ADR   155
Verbs in Court: Who Does What to Whom?   158

LATIN, JARGON . . . LEGALESE!

Latin Power for Fun   *167*
What's in a Name? Sometimes Everything   *168*
Legal Twosomes and Threesomes   *173*
Jargon: Lawyers' Shoptalk   *179*
Having to Do with . . .   *183*

PRACTICAL LEGALESE

How to Find a Lawyer   *187*
The Bottom Line   *190*

EPILOGUE   *195*

INDEX   *197*

ABOUT THE AUTHOR   *207*

COMMONLY USED SYMBOLS

Δ   **Defendant**

π   **Plaintiff**

K   **Contract**

THE
BASICS

LAWS WE KNOW INTUITIVELY

Many laws are complex and technical, and so is the special language associated with them. It is the main purpose of this book to explain some important areas of law and legalese. But let us start the ball rolling at a simpler level. Happily, there are principles of law that are truly obvious, based on childhood truths and commonsense adages. Below is a rather random collection of some of these truisms and examples of how they operate in the legal system.

1. If you don't speak up, you don't get. Or, as mother said, "The worst thing that can happen is that they'll say no." In law, as in life, silence may be interpreted as acquiescence. That is, if you don't speak up when something goes wrong or a transaction occurs, the other party may reasonably believe that you consented to whatever happened and may rely on that consent. There's even a word for this: *Lying by*. Following that you may be estopped (barred) from denying that the transaction occurred.

For example, the defense of condonation exists in fault divorce. This is a conditional pardon. If one spouse commits a marital offense known to the other spouse and they continue to cohabit, it is said that the other spouse has forgiven the offense by condonation.

If you receive a monthly bank statement that contains an error (such as a forgery or an error in summarizing your account) and you do nothing, after a while you may be said to have waived your right to correct it. Changes may be made later, but it may be much harder to make them.

Also, of course, all lawsuits are versions of this truism. When the plaintiff (π) begins a lawsuit, he is seeking a remedy from the defendant (Δ).

So you see, Mother was right again!

2. Possession is nine tenths of the law. The law generally favors keeping matters as they are; maintaining the status quo. All things being equal, a person in possession of something is more likely to keep it. A competitor for the object would have to prove that there is a need for change. This leads to another related truism: Don't fix it if it ain't broke! Leave well enough alone!

For instance, in a divorce situation, the parent with custody has a better chance of maintaining it than the other parent does in obtaining it. The house owner who keeps the last payment from the contractor until every last detail is completed to satisfaction knows this rule. Generally, it's easier to keep money than to fight for it—as the contractor may need to do.

3. It was only an accident! I didn't mean to. . . .

Kids say this all the time. They *know* it matters. In the law, for example, this principle appears all the time. Here's where children understand instinctively this fundamental basis of the American legal system: A person's intent is very important in determining the effect of lots of actions, from crimes to torts to contracts. Often, if it was "only an accident," the action may amount to negligence; if it was "on purpose" (intentional), it may be a crime.

4. First come, first served. Or, the early bird catches the worm. Or, he who hesitates is lost.

For example, if you have a security interest in someone's property, you have to protect that interest by perfecting it. This involves several steps, including providing notice—notifying all the world that you have a security interest in the property, the collateral. In this process it pays to be first, because the courts will use your date of perfection to give you priority over other perfected interest holders, should a dispute arise later. This process leads to the term "Race to the courthouse."

Then, too, there is the equitable principle of laches. You can't sleep on your rights. If you have a case you wish to pursue, you'd better do it! Don't wait too long. Otherwise, the other side may raise the defense of laches, as it would not be fair to permit you to go forward after you waited too long. On the other hand . . .

5. Let a sleeping dog lie. Leave well enough alone.

For instance, if enough time passes, the other side may not be able to sue you—may have exceeded the statute of limitations (see page 103), may provide you with the laches defense (see above), may simply run out of steam, or their best witness may disappear or . . . whatever!

6. Quit while you're ahead.

This principle is very important in negotiations. If you win a point, get it in writing and leave. Don't wait around for the other side to change its mind.

This leads to another adage . . .

7. There's many a slip between the cup and the lip.

For example, if you don't get it in writing, "signed, sealed, and delivered," lots of unexpected changes can happen in the meantime. This is roughly equivalent to Yogi Berra's famous slogan, "It ain't over till it's over."

8. It's not fair! Again, kids are right on the money! This oft-heard children's lament underlies the American legal system. From equal protection to due process the system is designed to assure as much fairness as possible. Then, too, remember there is the entire body of law called equity that has as its purpose the pursuit of fairness, the assurance of justice.

LAW AND EQUITY

Law is the set of rules enforced by society. Rules are enforced by authority, such as police, courts, and so on.

Equity is a system of justice administered according to standards of fairness (as opposed to standards imposed by specific laws or rules). Generally, equity follows the law. This means that applicable laws will be followed where they exist; where there are no applicable laws, principles of equity will be followed.

Since most of this book (and law books in general) focuses on *law,* these few pages will discuss equity.

1. Historically in England, sometimes enforcement of laws and legal rules was unfair or harsh because the rules were administered in an inflexible manner. That is, they were applied rigidly, even if the outcome was, in fact, unfair. To overcome this inflexibility, equity courts (also called courts of chancery) were established, based on broad principles of justice and fairness.

For example, it is unfair for one person to gain something of value at the expense of another. The equitable principle of unjust enrichment may require someone to restore goods or money to another person if not doing so would lead to an unfair result.

If a contractor is in the middle of building a house but stops, the equitable principle of *quantum meruit* requires that the house owner pay for the work already completed. There is no specific law that forces these payments. But it seems fair, doesn't it? It's a principle of fairness—thus, equity!

Today, in most states, law and equity courts are merged. In some states equity courts still exist. They may be called equity or courts of chancery.

2. Law courts generally deal with situations after damage has been done—for example, when a person's rights have been violated or a law has been broken.

In contrast equity courts may intervene to avoid damage, to prevent harm, and to promote fairness.

3. The main difference between law and equity courts lies in the relief they may order. Law courts may award money damages or punish wrongdoers. Equity courts deal with situations when money damages will not suffice. Sometimes the court may order a potential wrongdoer to stop doing something by issuing an injunction—for example, to stop dumping trash; or the court may order a person to do something through a mandatory injunction; or, perhaps, the court may order someone to stop doing an action for a brief period of time, by a TRO, a temporary restraining order—for example, an order to stop going to an ex-spouse's house.

Other equitable principles include unjust enrichment. (See above.) No one should unfairly gain over another party. Whatever such gains exist must be returned to the rightful owner.

Quantum meruit. (See above.) Paying for what has been earned; not getting away with not paying because of some later occurrence, such as a breach of K.

A court may order specific performance as an equitable remedy to a breach of K. That is, the court may order the party to do what he agreed to do, such as sell a sell a particular house or special antique to the buyer rather than simply pay money damages. The reason? There may be no other property just like it. Money damages alone would not suffice, would not "make the buyer whole."

The term *equity* is also used in the following situations: In a divorce a court may divide property between the spouses as the court believes to be fair, by equitable distribution, rather than by following specific rules, if that may lead to an unfair result.

Here's a test: Which is law and which is equity?

1. Judge awards fifty thousand dollars in damages to a family in a malpractice suit.
2. Judge orders Sam to sell his house to Bill.
3. Jane sues Tom for sending the wrong merchandise.
4. Mary seeks a court order to bar her ex-husband from her house.
5. Neighbors go to court to stop noisy Saturday-night parties down the street.

Answers:

1. law; 2. equity; 3. law; 4. equity; 5. equity.

CRIMINAL AND CIVIL LAWS: WHAT ARE THE DIFFERENCES?

Joe steals Bob's car. Car theft is a crime. Can this act result in a criminal case? or a civil case? Both! Here's how . . .

	CRIMINAL LAW	CIVIL LAW
DEFINITIONS	Deals with violations of existing laws. The government can prosecute Joe for car theft. Criminal law involves: —protecting citizens from law-breakers —providing constitutional and other rights for the accused —prosecuting (bringing to trial) the accused *Note:* A criminal act is considered a public wrong—an act against society. Even if there is only one victim, the government prosecutes the accused. (See page 129)	Deals with lawsuits to protect private rights. Here, Bob can sue Joe for compensation: that is, to repay him for his loss. (Usually, this is a sum of money.) *Note:* Civil law is considered to be private law because one person (a party) sues another. The government does not prosecute.
CAN THE SAME ACT INVOLVE BOTH CRIMINAL AND CIVIL LAWS?	YES. As in this case →	of Joe and Bob.

	CRIMINAL LAW	CIVIL LAW
WHO ARE THE PARTIES?	The government and the defendant(s) (Δ). It can be the state or federal government—depending on which laws are violated.	The π (injured party who files the complaint) and the Δ who answers it. A party can be one or more persons, a corporation, government, or large group of persons (as in a class action lawsuit).
WHAT IS THE ACTION CALLED?	*The People* v. *Joe* (v. means "versus," against) or *The State of XXX* v. *Joe* or *The U.S.* v. *Joe*	*Bob* v. *Joe* π v. Δ
WHAT ARE JOE'S AND BOB'S ROLES?	Joe is the Δ on trial. Bob is not a party but can be a prosecution witness (a witness for the government's case). *Note:* The district attorney or prosecuting attorney is the government's lawyer.	Bob is the π. Joe is the Δ.
CAN THE DEFENDANT BE PUNISHED?	YES. The government seeks to convict Joe (prove he is guilty) and to punish him.	NO. Generally, civil lawsuits seek to compensate the π; not to punish the Δ. Compensation is also called damages. *But note:* There are civil cases resulting in "punitive damages." Here the π gets more than compensatory damages; these are designed to punish the Δ for his wrongdoing, and make an example of him to others.
WHAT STANDARD OF PROOF IS NEEDED TO PREVAIL (WIN)?	BEYOND A REASONABLE DOUBT. The government must prove its case "to a moral certainty" to convict Joe. In a jury trial all jurors must agree (a unanimous verdict).	BY A PREPONDERANCE OF THE EVIDENCE. Bob has to prove his case against Joe is more likely true than not. In a jury trial the verdict need not be unanimous for Bob to prevail.

	CRIMINAL LAW	CIVIL LAW
IS IT A TRIAL BY JURY OR BY A JUDGE?	EITHER. The Constitution guarantees the accused a trial by a jury of his peers. (Sixth Amendment.) Over the years this right has been preserved for crimes punishable by more than six months in jail. The Δ may waive (give up) this right and request a trial by a judge.	EITHER. The Constitution guarantees the right to a jury. (Seventh Amendment.) Either party may choose a jury trial. However, the party that demands that right pays the jury fee.

LAWS, STATUTES, REGULATIONS, AND CANONS

My law is bigger than your law!

American law is an intricate combination of laws made by many different legislatures, including fifty states, one federal district (Washington, D.C.); the federal government; many court systems (state and federal), local governments, and a multitude of agencies and bureaus.

This has led to a hierarchical system of laws, with some laws more powerful than others. At the top of the hierarchy is the Constitution, of course.

Here's a chart of how this works. Note: The chart oversimplifies the situation; but it does give an idea of the hierarchy involved.

CONSTITUTION

FEDERAL STATUTES   STATE STATUTES   COMMON LAW*

FEDERAL REGULATIONS   STATE REGULATIONS

                           ORDINANCES

How does this work? For example, if two laws, one a state statute and another a federal statute, conflict (lead to different results), the federal statute controls (is followed). If a state regulation and a state statute conflict, the statute controls.

Now, things are not always so clear and simple, as you may imagine. Thus we have an area of law devoted to these types of questions, which is called, not surprisingly, *Conflicts!* Yes, Virginia, you may major in *Conflicts* in law school.

DEFINITIONS

Here are some definitions of various laws, rules, canons, et cetera.

1. U.S. Constitution: The document of fundamental principles of law, government, and freedoms by which our government operates. It was adopted in 1789 and has been amended twenty-six times since then.

2. State constitutions: All states have their own constitutions.

3. "Common law": Case law, court law. The common law (historically from England) is different from code/statutory law (historically from Napoleon's France and adopted in our own state of Louisiana). But in actuality

---

*The common law fills in where statutes leave gaps.
Courts interpret all of the above!

we now have a hybrid of the two systems: statutes by legislation; common law by courts.

Why would you care what a court says in a case about people you never heard of and will probably never meet? Because of the doctrine of precedence. Courts recognize earlier decisions as authority over later ones in the same jurisdiction. This means that courts tend to follow what earlier courts did in the same geographic or subject area. (See **Jurisdiction,** page 95.) The doctrine of precedence helps give a sense of predictability and stability to our laws. Courts can't do whatever they want with every case. Yes, there's even a fancy Latin word for this:

4. *Stare decisis:* Literally, "to stand by decided matters." Courts are reluctant to overrule precedents and, when they do, often do it in little steps, whittling away at the old case bit by bit. Watch what's happening with the abortion cases relating to *Roe* v. *Wade, Webster* v. *Reproductive Health Services,* and later cases.

Thus, if you live in Montana and are interested in a certain subject, say contracts (K's), you need to know how earlier Montana courts decided K cases similar to yours. That research will affect the rights and responsibilities you have in your case and will guide you in your strategy and preparation. If yours is a federal question, you'll be interested in how the federal courts, especially in your region, decided similar questions. (See **Jurisdiction,** page 95.)

5. Leading case: The most important case in a certain area of law. For example, in school desegregation it's *Brown* v. *Board of Education*.

6. Statutory law: Laws passed by legislatures, effective only in the *jurisdiction* of that legislature. For example, a Maine law is good in Maine. Once you cross over to another state, it has no effect. Young people know this too. That is why they drive over the border to a state with a lower age requirement to buy alcohol. On the other hand, a federal statute has effect in all fifty states, the District of Columbia, the territories, and so on.

7. Regulations: Written rules set up by federal or state administrative agencies to control, manage, and supervise specific matters over which those agencies have control and for which they can punish or sue violators. The agencies are established by legislatures, who, in effect, delegate to them the right to make regulations. This is an excellent example of the hierarchy in practice. If a conflict arises between the regulation and the statute that authorizes the regulation (the "enabling" legislation), the statute governs.

For example, the EPA (Environmental Protection Agency) regulations are designed to protect our air, water, and land. Anyone who disobeys them (pollutes the air, water, land) may be found in violation of EPA regulations. The FCC (Federal Communications Commission) regulations control and manage the airwaves (radio and television). The SEC (Securities and Exchange Commission) regulations are designed to control and manage the stock exchanges and financial systems in our country.

As our lives become more complex, more agencies are established with more regulations . . . so our lives become even more complex! And so it goes!

8. Doctrine: A government policy or principle of law that, while not written down in statute books, is nevertheless widely followed. (See the **doctrine of precedence,** page 13.)

9. Code: A systematic collection of laws.

For example, all federal laws are written in the USC (United States Code). Each state has a criminal code, a motor vehicle code, and so on. Business works under the UCC (Uniform Commercial Code), which has been adopted in whole or in part by all fifty states.

10. Canon: A rule, law, ordinance, church law. One example is the Canon of Judicial Ethics, which tells judges how to behave.

Note: Some of these terms are used interchangeably. For example, the judges' rules of conduct are called a canon, but lawyers' rules are a code: The Code of Professional Responsibility.

CITATION

How do you find these laws, statutes, regulations, and canons? A brief word about citations, the indexing system used in the law, by which you can find *any* case anywhere by simply knowing its name, which court it was heard in, or what page in a particular casebook it's on. The indexing system is truly beautiful. As many cases and courts as there are, each case is readily accessible to anyone.

For example, let's say you want to look up the 1973 abortion case *Roe* v. *Wade*. A citation is made up of the following categories of information:

NAME	VOLUME	NAME OF COURT*	PAGE	YEAR OF DECISION
Roe v. *Wade*	410	U.S. (Supreme Court)	133	(1973)

(Name of case is italicized) (First name is the PLAINTIFF, Roe; second name is the DEFENDANT, Wade; the v. is "VERSUS," meaning against. Thus, PLAINTIFF against the DEFENDANT.	π v. Δ *Roe* v. *Wade*, 410 U.S. 133 (1973).

*Many cases are reported by region, for example, NE (northeast), SW (southwest), and so on.

This is how the citation looks in a lawbook, a brief, anywhere! Go to any law library or even some large local libraries and see. Here's the later abortion case, *Webster* v. *Reproductive Health Services:* 57 U.S.L.W. 5023 (1989). Here's another famous case: *Brown* v. *Board of Education,* 347 U.S. 483 (1954). Just for fun, see if you can find it.

WHO IS A PERSON?

In the United States all persons have equal protection under the law. Who is a person? This question is easy to ask, but not so easy to answer. Disputes over the definition have been going on throughout our history and continue today on many fronts.

Logically, a person is a human being—male or female, adult or child. But legally, a person can also be a corporation.

The concept of personhood became important in 1868, after the Civil War, when the Fourteenth Amendment was ratified. Before that, slaves were not considered persons: in the Constitution they were considered three fifths of a person. The Fourteenth Amendment states, in part, ''nor shall any State deprive any person of life, liberty, or property, without due process of law; nor deny to any person within its jurisdiction the equal protection of the laws.'' Over the years Fourteenth Amendment definitions have been the basis of long and hard court fights.

So who is a person? And what is the equal protection of the laws? By now the following definitions have emerged—but they are always subject to change:

Not surprisingly, a person may be a human being, or a "natural person." Or an artificial person, such as a corporation, a labor union, or another organization.

But, contrary to popular belief, not all human beings are persons for all purposes. An illegitimate child is a person under the Fourteenth Amendment and the wrongful-death statutes of all the states, but may not be under all inheritance laws. Thus an illegitimate child may not inherit from his father through intestacy unless he is legitimized. See state law—this is a rapidly changing area of law.

An illegitimate child is a child born at a time his parents are not married to each other. If his parents marry between the time he is conceived and the time he is born, he is considered legitimate. Legitimation is the court procedure by which an illegitimate child becomes legitimate.

Courts and society are now grappling with this question: Is an unborn child a person under the Fourteenth Amendment? At what stage of fetal development, if any, does that unborn child become a "person"? See, for example, the 1973 Supreme Court decision *Roe* v. *Wade*. (See page 15.) A fetus is an unborn child between the eighth week after conception until birth. Before the eighth week the emerging child is generally called an "embryo."

Thus it's the battle over the definition of *person* that underlies part of the current abortion struggle. If a fetus is a person, then he is entitled to equal protection of the laws and the right to life. Then, from a legal standpoint, there can be no abortion. If he is not a person, then there is no such entitlement to equal protection. Competing interests can prevail, such as the woman's right to privacy or freedom of choice.

In legal terms there are also several levels of fetal development, each with its own consequences. For example, a viable unborn child is a fetus that would have been born but for the negligence of someone. Hence, a viable unborn child is a person under the wrongful-death statutes. If a fetus dies in a car accident or through medical malpractice, his parent may sue the negligent driver or doctor for damages under the wrongful-death statutes.

Wrongful-death statutes are laws, observed in all states and by the federal government, that permit an executor, an administrator, or an heir to sue for damages when someone dies because of negligence by another person. (See **Wills,** page 54.) These statutes changed the common law, by which a person's rights died when he did.

The law classifies people in other ways, also. Each of us is either competent or incompetent. Adults are competent, unless they have been judged incompetent by a court because of mental disability or other infirmity. Children—minors—are incompetent.

Why does the law divide people like this? Our laws deal with people in their capacity to be responsible for themselves and their actions. Thus only legally competent people may be held responsible in the many different civil and criminal matters of modern life.

You can't be guilty of a crime if you were incompetent at the time. You can't sign a contract (**K**) if you do not have legal capacity to consent to the **K**. Then there is the related concept of "competency to stand trial" in a criminal case. This has to do with the defendant's (**Δ's**) *present* ability to understand the proceedings, consult with his attorney, and aid in his defense.

These terms and concepts are explained below.

Age of minority refers to a person who is a child, or a minor; that is, someone below the age of majority or the age of consent. This age is usually eighteen, though it differs from state to state. Also, different rights may emerge at different ages in any state. For example, an eighteen-year-old has the right to vote, but may not be able to drink or marry.

Age of majority refers to an adult; that is, someone over the age of majority. An adult is legally able to take care of himself.

Mental incompetency, which is determined by a court, refers to an adult who has been judged unable to care for himself due to mental disability or unfitness.

A child has no legal capacity to be an adult. This is because a minor is below the legal age of consent. The law states that a minor cannot agree to anything binding. He cannot buy property, enter into a K, marry without parental consent, write a will, or take other actions that can legally be done by an adult.

An incompetent adult's rights depend on the court order involved and the relevant state statutes. For example, some may marry; others may not.

Because of this "incompetency," if a minor enters into a K, it may be voidable. If a minor engages in sexual intercourse with someone "over the age of consent," the adult can present no evidence that will rebut the law's presumption that a minor cannot consent to sexual intercourse. Since an important defense for rape is consent, the accused may have no fact to rebut (contradict) the presumption. The rape involved is called "statutory rape." Statutory rape is based on an irrebuttable presumption—that is, a legal conclusion that can't be contradicted by any facts.

An irrebuttable presumption also exists that a *very young child* cannot commit a crime. (The age differs from state to state, but it's usually around seven.) Thus, if a young child commits an act that would be criminal if committed by an adult, he cannot be charged with that crime because of the irrebuttable presumption. Again, check local laws!

The minor's parents are his legal guardians unless a court appoints someone else. An adult is his own legal guardian. The court appoints a legal guardian for an incompetent, or ward. (See below.)

The following definitions of parents and children are based on common law. But many of these relationships are evolving and changing by statutes. When in doubt, check local law on any of these matters!

A child has rights to the support, care, and protection of his parents. A parent has the responsibility to provide support, care, and protection for his child. Usually, when a child reaches the age of majority, a parent's duty of support ends. Sometimes, however, it continues, particularly for educational expenses. A parent may be obligated to pay his (adult) child's college bills! This is spelled out often in divorce settlements and cases.

A child is subject to the control and supervision of his parent. He has to obey them. A parent has the right to a child's obedience, and, under common law, the right to all the earnings of his minor child.

Because of this duty to obey, a child is subject to status offenses that would not be crimes if committed by an adult. These offenses include truancy (not attending school), running away from home, and disobeying parents (also known as being an incorrigible child). Alternatively, because of the parent's duty to support, protect, and care for a child, a parent who breaches that duty may be found guilty of neglect or abuse.

Since so much in the law is a balancing of rights, the flip side of this part of law asserts that a child who commits a crime may be charged in Juvenile Court as a juvenile offender or juvenile delinquent for a crime that normally would be an adult crime. Usually, juvenile courts treat minors in a less punitive manner, with more emphasis on early rehabilitation. The law in this field is constantly evolving.

Often when a minor commits a heinous crime, you may read that the prosecutor seeks to have the juvenile tried as an adult, to avoid these protections.

On the other hand (in law, there is always another hand!), if a minor engages in an adult activity, he may be charged as an adult. Take driving, for example. The law presumes that anyone who drives consents to obey the rules of the road. This includes minors. Clearly, this is inconsistent, since minors are not competent and can't consent! But there it is. It's hard to have it both ways.

When a parent is guilty of abuse or neglect, why can the state remove the child from the parent? Ah, because of the concept of *parens patriae*! The state is considered the parent of us all, the "superparent." Legally, the state places a child in his parent's care. If the parent does a fine job, all is well. If the parent neglects or abuses the child, the state may exercise its right/duty of *parens patriae* and intervene to protect the child. The concept of *parens patriae* is very important in understanding much of modern-day social welfare law.

Emancipation: A minor may become emancipated either by reaching the age of majority or by demonstrating his independence. This may be through marriage, by joining the armed services, or by moving out of the house and being self-supporting. Local law may differ on this one!

If a child becomes emancipated, the parent's duties of support and care usually end. Again, state laws differ here. Check them!

Finally, we get to answer the question: Who is a parent legally? And are there different types of "parent"?

Basically, there are two types of parent: natural and adoptive. Generally speaking, a natural parent is the mother or father to whom a child is born. These definitions used to be easy, but with test-tube babies, *in vitro* fertilization, surrogate mothers, and other complexities related to modern science, they are far more problematic. Sometimes it's hard to know who is the father or mother of a child. Sometimes there is more than one of each! This situation presents a clear example of the law's challenge to keep up with science and adapt its definitions to changing times.

An adoptive parent adopts a child through a court action. Adoption is a court proceeding that establishes the relation of parent and child for people who are not the natural parents. The adoption process substitutes adoptive parent(s) for natural parent(s).

Remember that parental rights may end only by court order, and they may start, as in adoption, only by court order.

Traditionally, the term *parent* does not include the following:

Stepparent: A person married to a child's parent who has not adopted the child. In old common law a stepparent had no legal obligation to support or care for a child. Now, by statute in many states, this is changing.

Foster parent: A person who performs parental duties of care, supervision, and support for a child not his own. Usually, a foster parent is appointed by a state agency and is paid the child's expenses. Generally, a foster parent has physical, but not legal, custody of the child.

Surrogate parent (the old definition; not the surrogate mother who carries a baby to term for someone else): A person who voluntarily assumes the rights and responsibilities of a parent, without the legal title. A surrogate is a substitute. He or she may also be someone appointed by a court to make educational decisions for a child.

Grandparent: A parent of a child's parents. A grandparent used to have no legal rights relating to a grandchild. But there are cases now in which a grandparent is given visitation rights and sometimes other legal rights in a divorce situation.

As times change, so does the law.

Here are some related terms:

Guardian or legal guardian: Someone appointed by a court to care for a minor or an incompetent adult and, in some cases, for his property or estate. The minor or incompetent adult is called the ward.

Guardian ad litem: Someone appointed by a court to investigate a case from the ward's perspective and to protect a ward's rights and interests in a specific legal proceeding.

Conservator: Someone appointed by a court to care for an incompetent's property. This is a less drastic measure than a guardianship.

Next friend: Someone who volunteers to protect the

rights of a minor or incompetent adult in a legal proceeding. This person is not court appointed but acts as a "court officer" or "agent."

The following terms do not involve court actions.

Power of attorney: A document or instrument by which a person appoints someone to perform certain acts for him, such as writing checks, taking funds from bank accounts, or paying bills. The appointer is called the "principal"; the appointed, the "agent" or "attorney" appointed by the document. The instrument is evidence to all third parties that the attorney is authorized to act for the principal. For example, if you are a bank teller, it's okay to give the attorney money from the principal's account—once you verify the power of attorney.

Note: The term *attorney,* as used here, does not mean "lawyer" or "attorney at law." It means agent. Of course a "lawyer" may be appointed to serve this function.

The power of attorney ends upon the death of the principal.

Durable power of attorney: Same as above, except that it is effective when the principal becomes incapacitated or disabled. The durable power of attorney is created by state statutes and differs from state to state.

CIVIL LAW
AND
LAWSUITS

TORTS

Funny word. In French (where it originated) a *tort* means "wrong." But in the U.S. most people probably think it means a chocolate cake with icing, when they think of it at all! A torte! But, alas, no.

A TORT IS A CIVIL WRONG

Tort law is part of civil (noncriminal) law. It concerns lawsuits (not prosecutions). These suits arise from injuries (wrongs) committed by one person or a group or organization against another or others. Torts can be intentional or not. They can be purposeful or negligent.

Here's what happens. You get hurt. Someone treats you badly, unfairly. You want to "sue the bastards." Tort law answers the question: Is there someone to sue?

Or, putting it in legalese, is there a remedy for every tort? Torts deal with civil lawsuits, excluding breaches of contract (K's). While torts are not part of criminal law, remember that the same action by a defendant (Δ) can bring about both a criminal prosecution and a civil lawsuit.

For example, if Bill steals your TV, that's the crime of theft. It is also the tort of conversion.

The district attorney can prosecute for the theft. You can sue for the conversion.

Bill is the tort-feasor (doer of the tort!). With this as background, what are some torts?

TYPES OF TORTS

Torts are divided into basic types:

1. Negligence
2. Intentional harm to a person
3. Intentional harm to tangible property
4. Strict liability
5. Nuisance
6. Harm to economic interests
7. Harm to intangible property interests

1. NEGLIGENCE

Negligence includes car accidents, slip-and-fall cases, malpractice, personal injury, some product liability cases. The variety of negligence is very wide, and new torts are created all the time.

While it is a common word, *negligence* has legal meaning. What is it? How does negligence become a tort?

We start from the idea that negligence is carelessness, not being reasonable, et cetera.

Here's how a tort in negligence is analyzed. Every tort has three elements:

A. The Δ owes a legal duty to the plaintiff (π).
B. The Δ breaches that duty.
C. The breach causes injury either as a direct result of the negligent act or somewhat more indirectly, but foreseeably; that is, the injury was reasonably predictable following the negligent act.

Legally, we say there is a proximate cause between the breach and the injury.

These look like simple words—not too technical. But let's define what they mean in this context.

First, what is a duty? One person's obligation to another. Duty is based on the relationship of the people involved.

For example:

> employer and employee
>
> innkeeper and guest
>
> business person/owner and customer
>
> host and social visitor
>
> manufacturer and consumer
>
> property owner and licensee or guest or trespasser or trespasser who is younger than twelve years old
>
> person in control of an instrument that can harm (e.g., a car) and a passenger or pedestrian or fellow driver

In all these cases there is a different standard of care, of duty. It's different if the mailman slips on your steps or if a trespasser does.

But, basically, the duty is to act reasonably.

What is reasonable? (Ah, the sixty-four-thousand-dollar question!)

Reasonable conduct: An important concept in tort law but, as you can imagine, hard for π's and Δ's to agree upon. Lawyers use the "reasonable person standard." What would a reasonable person do?

Note: You generally don't have a duty to a stranger. Thus, as harsh as it may be, if you see a stranger in serious trouble, you don't have a duty to help. However, laws are changing in this field.

In fact, if you help, you better be reasonable! Because, by helping, you assume a duty!

Good Samaritan statutes: Because it seems harsh to let doctors, nurses, and other medical professionals go about their way without helping strangers in distress, many states have enacted Good Samaritan statutes. The name comes from the Bible. These laws protect from lawsuits doctors and other medical professionals who aid an injured stranger in an emergency at the scene of an accident or injury. The duty of reasonable care does not apply. In such a case the π can sue the doctor (Δ) only if he was reckless or grossly negligent.

The reasonable person standard is an objective, not subjective, standard. A jury can decide if *you* were reasonable. "I was doing the best I could" or "I thought I was being reasonable" are not defenses if they do not meet the community's reasonableness standard.

Standards are applied to the type of person you are. A reasonable adult. A reasonable lawyer. A reasonable scientist or shopkeeper. Persons with greater knowledge are held to a higher standard.

The reasonableness standard does not apply to children unless they are doing adult activities. Thus, if a sixteen-year-old drives a car, he had better be reasonable.

These standards change all the time. For example, right now the community's standard for drinking and driving is changing dramatically in this country. It used to be viewed as almost funny; now, you'd better not do it, you'd better have a "designated driver" if you're planning to go out and drink, and on and on . . . All these new standards are being applied differently than they were twenty or even ten years ago. . . .

Next, what is a breach? It is a failure to act reasonably; a failure to use the amount of care a reasonable person would use in that situation.

Negligence occurs if you do something below the standard of what a reasonable person would do in those circumstances. What's the measure? A community standard or statute.

Let's say that you are careless with someone to whom you owe a duty. Is that a tort?

Not necessarily. Not unless the person is hurt by your negligence. If no one got hurt, you got lucky!

Finally, what is causation? Something that causes something else. To figure out if there is the required causation in your case, you have to analyze it in several steps.

1. You have to prove a "but for" relation between the breach of duty and the injury. *But for* the breach, there would be no injury. For example, the floor in the store is slippery. You fall on it and break a bone. The slippery floor probably caused your fall.

If π gets hurt but the injury was not caused by Δ's action, then there is no tort. For example, you are in the store with your child. He runs away from you. You run after him and fall and break a bone. The floor was not slippery. The floor probably did not cause your fall. Probably no negligence on the store's part.

2. The injury has to be the direct result of the negligent act or of foreseeable intervening forces. The injury has to be caused proximately by the breach of duty. This means it has to be reasonably anticipated that if someone does X, someone can get hurt. If you drive and drink, you may cause an injury. If there is a banana peel on the floor in the store, someone may fall, et cetera. This is the proximate cause requirement.

If something else happens between the breach and the injury, it's hard to prove that the breach caused the injury. For example, if your neighbor takes down a wall and water comes into your basement as a result, it may be a tort. But if water doesn't come in for five years, it's harder to prove proximate cause because so many other things intervened during the five years. Or if there is an unusual flood up the street at the same time as the wall was removed, your neighbor may be able to prove that it was the flood, not the wall, that caused the water in your basement. That might be what's termed "an act of God." Then you have no one to sue!

Other important terms in negligence torts:

Invitee: Someone you have, expressly or by implication, invited to your property. He may be a customer, servant, friend. Generally, it is your responsibility to exercise reasonable care for his safety against latent defects on that part of your property to which he was invited. (See **Legal Twosomes and Threesomes,** page 173.) In addition you have a duty to make reasonable inspections to discover dangerous conditions and, thereafter, make them safe.

For example, in a store, the invitees can come into the selling area but not the back, which is posted "FOR EMPLOYEES ONLY." There they would be trespassers. (See definition below.)

Licensee: A person who comes onto your property with permission, but without invitation. Such a person has a right to be there but is there for his benefit, not yours: for example, a door-to-door salesman.

In the old common law you owed these folks less duty of care. Now, by statute in many states, the duty is the same as for invitees.

Trespasser: Someone on your property without invitation or license; someone who commits a trespass on your property. (See page 35.) Generally, you owe him less care than an invitee or licensee but will be responsible for conduct that is grossly negligent. Thus you can't set an unmarked trap or leave a large unprotected hole on your property.

An exception is for children under twelve years old. You may be held responsible in their case for maintaining an attractive nuisance—a dangerous "artificial condition" on your property that a child may play on. If the child gets hurt, you may be liable, even if he is trespassing. For example, a swimming pool with an open gate or no fence at all. On the other hand, a tree the child climbs is probably not an "artificial condition," and you'd probably not be liable for an injury.

Res ipsa loquitur: Lovely Latin term you must know if you plan to speak to a lawyer. Keep it in your back pocket just for fun! Literally, this doctrine means "the thing *(res)* speaks *(loquitur)* for itself *(ipsa)*." It's used in trying to prove that the Δ was negligent. Here, one can infer negligence without actually proving it, if (a) the accident would not have happened without negligence and (b) the Δ had exclusive control of the thing that injured the π. If the doctrine applies, the π has made a *prima facie* case and the jury cannot give a directed verdict for the Δ. (See **Standard of Proof,** page 101.)

Product liability: A manufacturer and seller of a defective product may be liable in negligence. In some cases they are liable also in strict liability. (See page 35.)

Now for the other types of torts listed on page 28:

2. INTENTIONAL HARM TO A PERSON

A. Assault: The Δ intends to hurt or scare the π and the π believes he is in danger of being hurt *at that moment*.

If I point a gun at you and it scares you, that's an assault, even if it turns out to be a toy gun.

If I say, "Don't you ever do that again or I'll kill you," that is not an assault: words alone don't do it. Here there is no immediate threat of harm.

In an assault the Δ does not need to touch the π.

B. Battery: The Δ intends to offensively touch or hurt the π without the π's consent, and does so.

Even if the π is asleep, and the Δ offensively touches him, that's a battery—because it was without consent.

When you sign a medical release before surgery, you are, in effect, consenting to the doctor's touching you. If he does the surgery to which you consented, that's not a battery. If he does more or different surgery, that may be a battery—because he went beyond the scope of consent.

Complicated, isn't it?

C. False imprisonment: The Δ intends to keep the π from freely moving about in an area that the π can't leave. If I'm driving my car with you in it, and you want to get out, and I don't stop, that may be false imprisonment. An intentional tort.

If a storekeeper keeps me on the suspicion of shoplifting, that may be false imprisonment, if his suspicion was unreasonable.

D. Intentional mental distress: The Δ intentionally or recklessly causes π severe emotional distress.

If I know you are petrified of snakes and I leave one in your desk, that may be grounds for a suit based on intentional infliction of emotional/mental distress.

3. INTENTIONAL HARM TO TANGIBLE PROPERTY

A. Trespass to land: An intrusion by Δ onto π's land. No harm or intent needs to be proven. For example, if your neighbor builds a fence but it happens to sit on part of your property, that's a trespass, even if he did it unintentionally.

B. Trespass to chattels: The Δ interferes with π's right to possess his property. For example, the Δ takes π's property, uses it, perhaps damages it.

C. Conversion: An act that interferes with the owner's use of his property. Basically, it's the tort version of the crime of theft or destruction of property, which is serious enough so that the Δ should pay its full value to the π.

4. STRICT LIABILITY

If injured, the π does not need to prove any negligence on the Δ's part. With products he must prove that the product was not safe for its intended use and that he was injured by it.

The duty to warn is often applied to potentially dangerous products. For example, crash-worthiness of cars; hazards and side effects of medications. This is why cigarettes have warning labels. Even ladders now have warning signs on them! Are the products safe for their intended use?

Ultrahazardous activity: Owning certain types of animals, or engaging in certain types of activities. For example, firearms, if not commonly fired in the particular community or area. If anyone gets hurt, the Δ may be liable, even if he was not negligent.

5. NUISANCE

The Δ unreasonably interferes with the π's enjoyment of his property. This is where the neighbor's noisy parties come in! Or unsavory odors. Or flights overhead. Courts balance the type of area you are in, the nature of the harm, and the social value/utility of that activity. Airplanes must fly but parties can be quieter.

6. HARM TO ECONOMIC INTERESTS

A. Deceit: Occurs if the Δ knowingly lies about an important fact that he intends to induce the π to rely on and which, in fact, the π does rely on. For example, right before trying to sell his house, the Δ patches over evidence of major water damage so that potential buyers can't see the damage.

B. Negligent misrepresentation: It's like deceit, but applies to people in their trade or business or profession. It occurs if the Δ negligently provides false information to the π, a customer, on which the π relies to his detriment.

C. **Interference with contractual relationships:**
The Δ intentionally interferes with an ongoing business relationship between the π and someone else (the third party).

D. **Intentional interference with advantageous relations:** The Δ interferes through tortious means (duress, fraud) where he had no business being in the first place. For example, the Δ fraudulently induces a change in a testator's will in which the π was to be a beneficiary.

7. HARM TO INTANGIBLE PROPERTY INTERESTS

A. **Defamation:** Occurs if Δ communicates information about π to others which is not truthful and hurts the π's reputation. If the Δ was negligent, in not doing enough research or background checks, he may be liable.

Libel: If the defamation occurs in writing.
Slander: If the defamation is spoken.

With famous people, public officials, or other people in the "public domain," only defamation done with malice (ill will) may be a tort.

B. **Malicious prosecution:** If the π starts a criminal prosecution against the Δ without probable cause and with malice and the Δ wins, he may turn around and sue the π for malicious prosecution.

C. **Invasion of privacy:** A wrongful intrusion into a person's private life, whether by others or by the government.

For example, such an invasion may occur if unreasonable publicity is given to someone's private life. "It's not anyone else's business!'' If someone takes your name or uses your picture without permission, especially for commercial use, that may be such an invasion. The computer revolution has brought the right to privacy to the fore: How much may government, industry, and other institutions lawfully know about us? Also, the current abortion fight is about this right, at least in part. Do the abortion laws invade the woman's privacy? So the ''right to privacy,'' which, contrary to popular belief, does not appear in the Constitution in so many words, is all around us!

And there you have them: many of the major torts that exist in the 1990s. Stay tuned as new ones emerge to meet changing social, economic, and personal needs. . . . The law is ever-changing and organic.

CONTRACTS (K's)

Let's go for it! It's a deal! A meeting of the minds.

Contracts happen all the time. They are everywhere! How many did you participate in today?

Did you shop in a store? ride the bus? buy a car? eat at a restaurant? work at your job? attend a movie?

Why are these common everyday events **K**'s? In each, one party makes an offer requiring consideration that the other accepts. For example, the store displays goods for sale (an offer) that the buyer wants and pays (acceptance) for (consideration): Voilà! There's a **K**.

What is a **K**?

It's an agreement between two or more parties that requires each to do or give something in exchange. Once made, it is enforceable in court. In an important way it's an example of people making their own laws—within the guidelines established by statute, courts, and tradition.

In most cases, **K**'s involve the exchange of goods or services for money.

Below is a flow chart of the life of a **K**, followed by definitions of the legal terms in chronological order. (The numbers refer back to the flow chart above.)

LIFE OF A CONTRACT

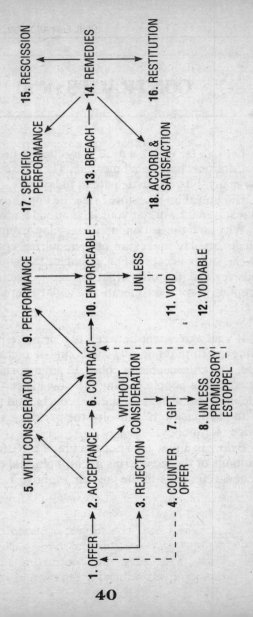

40

1. OFFER

An action or indication by one party (the offeror) that he is willing to make an agreement with another party (the offeree), which, if accepted, will create a K. A demonstration (manifestation) of the intent to make a deal.

The manifestation can be in many forms: spoken or written or displayed. When you walk into a restaurant and sit down, the owner offers to feed you and you indicate your acceptance by sitting down, ordering your meal, and eating it. Not a word about K's is spoken! But you've entered into one. You've clearly demonstrated—manifested—your intentions.

Another example of an offer: "I (offeror) will sell you (offeree) my car for three thousand dollars."

Example of a non-offer: "I am thinking of selling my car for three thousand dollars." Even if you say you'll pay me the three thousand there's no K because I never offered to sell it!

An offer needs four specific and definite terms: the who, the what, the price, the time.

The who: Both parties must have the mental capacity to make a K. That is, they should be adults with the ability to understand what they are doing. (Contracts made with children or mentally incompetent adults are not covered in these materials. They are generally voidable. See below.) (See **Who Is a Person?**, page 16 and below, page 46.)

The what: The subject of the offer must be definite and specific and both parties should know what they are contracting about. If I thought I was selling the red car and you thought you were buying the blue one, there may be no deal. This is the mutuality requirement of **K**'s. Lawyers talk about the "meeting of the minds." Parties have to agree about the same thing and the same terms.

The price: The price or other consideration must be definite and specific.

The time: the offeror specifies the length of time the offer remains open. For example, "If I don't hear from you by Friday, the deal's off." If no time is specified, the law implies a reasonable period of time, depending on circumstances.

2. ACCEPTANCE

An offeree's agreeing to the terms of the offer. "Yes, I'll buy that car for three thousand dollars next week." Your sitting down at the restaurant is an acceptance. Remember: silence can be a form of acceptance. (See **Laws We Know Intuitively,** page 3.)

3. REJECTION

An offeree's non-acceptance of the terms of the offer, either by an outright rejection or by a counteroffer.

4. COUNTEROFFER

A change in the offer made by the offeree. For example, "I'll buy your car for twenty-five hundred dollars," or "I'll buy your car if you wash it." This is not an acceptance; it's a counteroffer. It does not create a **K**. Rather, it creates a new offer, this time by the (former) offeree.

5. CONSIDERATION

Something of value exchanged for a promise or performance. "I'll pay you twenty dollars for mowing my lawn." Usually, consideration is required to make the promise binding and the **K** enforceable in court. It's the *quid pro quo* ("something for something") of the deal. In this case twenty dollars and the mowing are the mutual considerations.

6. CONTRACT (**K**)

In its simplest definition it's an agreement between two or more parties. Each makes a promise that, if breached, is enforceable in court.

Contrary to popular belief, **K**'s may be written or oral. So long as there is an offer, an acceptance, consideration, and other terms are satisfied (e.g., the parties have the required mental capacity, the subject of the **K** is not illegal, and so on), there can be an enforceable **K**, whether written or not.

But some specific **K**'s must be in writing to be enforceable. These include:

A. **K**'s dealing with real estate, except for a lease for less than a year.

B. **K**'s for the sale of goods for more than five hundred dollars.

C. **K**'s for a job that lasts more than one year.

D. **K**'s in consideration of marriage, such as prenuptial agreements.

E. **K**'s that promise to pay someone's debts.

In general, and for these **K**'s in particular, an important reason to "get it in writing" is that a writing memorializes the transaction. Memory can fail. If an argument arises later about any aspect of the K, the parties can prove their positions more easily if they are written down. "But you said . . . ," "No, I didn't," or "Gee, I don't remember," aren't very persuasive.

7. GIFT

A promise of performance given without anything of value in exchange. Usually, gifts or the promise of gifts are unenforceable.

Exception: A gift may be deemed a K under certain situations, in a quasi-K. The law may imply a K in order to promote fairness and justice. Unlike an explicit (actual) K it is not based on the parties' mutual intent. Rather, it's based on the principle that a party has to pay for what he receives. (See **Law and Equity,** page 6.)

For example, if a stranger finds your dog and feeds him for several days before you find the stranger and your dog, a K for the room and board for the dog may be created. Besides being grateful for the return of your "best friend," you may have to pay for his care.

Did anyone say this would be easy? It may not be easy, but there is a certain beauty and fairness in it, isn't there? We move on!

8. PROMISSORY ESTOPPEL

An equitable (equity) doctrine that makes a promise binding, even if there was no consideration, if that is the only way to promote justice.

For example: Uncle Bob promises nephew Jim one thousand dollars after he graduates. Jim spends the money on a new TV before he actually gets the money. Later, Uncle Bob doesn't pay. If Jim's reliance on the promise was reasonable (Uncle Bob had kept his promises in the past!), then Uncle Bob may be estopped (prevented) from denying the existence of a K, even though, in fact, one had not been made. (Uncle Bob had, in fact, simply promised a gift.) The promise may be enforced, up to the amount already spent—the amount relied upon. These cases rely on the facts: Was the reliance reasonable? Did Jim graduate? Et cetera.

9. PERFORMANCE

The putting into effect of what the K specifies; the enactment of what's promised, whether to buy a car, paint a house, start work for the other party, et cetera.

10. ENFORCEABLE

A K that the law will enforce. You may take a K to court to seek a remedy if you believe the K was breached. Obviously, whether you win or not depends on the facts you present.

11. VOID K

A K, though it may have the necessary terms, is not enforceable.

For example: An agreement to do an illegal act, such as to kill a person, or to buy contraband or to pay gambling debts (unless in a jurisdiction where gambling is legal), is void. It was never an enforceable K. Another fancier way to state this: It was *null and void ab initio*. It had no value from the beginning.

12. VOIDABLE K

A **K** that may be canceled by one side. For example, a **K** with a minor may be voidable, if the minor chooses to cancel it. The minor may choose to do this at any time while he is still a minor. If he doesn't cancel it, then it may be enforced. (See page 16.)

A **K** that is grossly unfair to one side (generally a consumer) may be voided by a court (not the parties themselves). This is an equity principle, codified under the Uniform Commercial Code (UCC). It may be voided because it would be unfair, unconscionable, to enforce it. (See page 6.) This is an example of the doctrine of unconscionability.

Other voidable **K**'s are those made by an unintentional mistake or through intentional fraud or misrepresentation or duress. Again, the dispute becomes a factual one.

13. BREACH

A failure to carry out the terms of the contract. In legalese, it's "wrongful nonperformance."

14. REMEDIES

When a breach occurs, remedies are used to right the wrong, to compensate the party whose **K** was breached. Remedies in *law* and *equity* include:

15. RESCISSION

The cancellation of a **K** and the returning of the parties to their situation before the **K**, the *status quo ante*. The parties, not performing the

K, may have to return items or moneys exchanged. This type of returning is called "restitution"—returning things to the owner to "make him whole," as he was before the **K**, so there is no unjust enrichment by either party. This is an equity principle. The law does not like one party taking an unfair advantage of another. In equitable terms it's simply not fair! (See page 6.)

16. RESTITUTION

See **rescission** above.

17. SPECIFIC PERFORMANCE

Forcing one party to perform according to the **K**. This remedy may exist in real estate cases, where a seller may be forced to sell the property to the buyer. The theory is that this is the only way to make the buyer whole, as no two properties are the same. Usually, you can't force a person to perform a job or service. That's slavery! It was outlawed after the Civil War by the Thirteenth Amendment!

Isn't it interesting how these various laws merge and interplay? Yes, what we learned in civics actually works!

18. ACCORD AND SATISFACTION

The parties may agree to settle for less than bargained for in the **K**. This is a type of forgiveness. In effect a new **K** is entered into. For example, the buyer might accept the goods later than promised without demanding a penalty.

MARRIAGE AND DIVORCE: THE BASICS

GETTING TOGETHER

Marriage is a **K**. John and Mary promise to fulfill the duties of a married couple as imposed by law. These include support, inheritance, and *consortium*. Consortium is the legal right of one spouse to the company and affection of the other.

John and Mary marry after fulfilling the state's requirements (including age and mental competence), obtaining a license, passing blood tests, and having a ceremony with witnesses. Their marriage is a "special" **K** because John and Mary cannot dissolve (end) it. Only a court can do that.

Common law Marriage: If John and Mary live in a state that recognizes this type of marriage, they may enter into it as follows: They can live together (cohabit); and they can "hold themselves out" as if they were married, by telling others they are married and referring to themselves as married people. Common law marriages do not require ceremonies or licenses. And contrary to popular belief, the cohabitation period need not always be as long as seven years. It varies from state to state.

Prenuptial agreement: Also called premarital or antenuptial agreement: A **K** that two people may write and agree upon. It details their rights and duties, especially with respect to property and debts. The goal of a prenuptial agreement is to minimize future disputes in case of divorce or when one spouse dies.

Living together: From a general legal standpoint this arrangement is not a marriage. John and Mary live together. Period. Recently, however, some states have held that *express* or *implied* agreements between John and Mary during their life together are enforceable after they break up. (See **palimony,** p. 52.)

SPLITTING UP

Separation: A legal term that refers to John and Mary's agreement to live apart although they are married. They may enter into an agreement about all the aspects of their separation.

Note that if John or Mary later *breaches* their agreement, the court will treat it as a *breach of* **K**.

Legal separation: A legal term that refers to a court order. If John and Mary cannot agree on terms of a separation, either of them may sue the other in court. If the court orders the terms of separation, the order is a "legal separation." It may also be called "temporary orders."

Note that if John or Mary later breaches this order, the breach will be treated as *contempt of court.*

Desertion, or abandonment: The legal result of John's or Mary's leaving the other without an agreement between them. Desertion is a ground, or legal cause, of fault divorce. Check state law, as each has a different description of what constitutes desertion.

Remember that laws of marriage and divorce are established by the states because of the Tenth Amendment to the Constitution. This amendment reserves to the state or people all powers not delegated by the

Constitution to the federal government. There is no federal marriage and divorce law.

DIVORCE—DISSOLUTION—ANNULMENT

Divorce or dissolution: The end of a marriage by *court decree. Dissolution* is the term more often used in *no-fault* actions. Following a divorce, John's and Mary's rights and duties are specified from the date of the *final decree.*

Annulment: A court decree stating that John and Mary never legally married because they didn't fulfill the requirements of marriage. Perhaps John or Mary fraudulently deceived the other.

Following an annulment, John and Mary revert to their premarital status. They are single, have never been married.

Fault divorce: What may result if John or Mary sues the other for divorce, claiming that the spouse is "at fault." Note that the fault needs to be proven.

Different grounds of fault include:

—adultery
—bigamy
—conviction of a crime involving *moral turpitude* (an act that is so vile—or base—that it contravenes basic moral standards)
—cruelty (mental or physical)
—desertion or abandonment
—habitual drunkenness
—insanity
—nonsupport

Contested divorce: If John and Mary cannot agree on the terms of their divorce. Their case will be argued, or contested, in court.

Uncontested or default divorce: When John and Mary agree on the terms or one of them does not appear in court. The court finalizes the agreement or default.

No-fault divorce or dissolution: A divorce that is decreed in a state with *no-fault* divorces. In this type of divorce couples may be able to meet the *standards of proof* easily.

A marriage can be ended for the following reasons, or grounds:

—irreconcilable differences that have led to an irretrievable breakdown of the marriage (John and Mary cannot get along).
—separation for a specified time.

Quickie divorce: What occurs if John or Mary goes to a state or country with a short residency requirement for divorce for the purpose of obtaining the divorce.

This kind of divorce dissolves the marriage only. It cannot deal with custody or property issues, because that state or country has no jurisdiction over those issues. (See **Jurisdiction,** page 95.)

ISSUES IN A DIVORCE/ DISSOLUTION ACTION

Alimony: Money for support and maintenance to which one spouse is entitled from the other spouse after a divorce or separation. (See **palimony** below.)

The court usually awards an amount based on need.

Payments often end if the receiving spouse remarries or if either spouse dies.

Palimony: Support (money) that may be awarded to John or Mary, even if unmarried, after they stop living together. (They must have had an enforceable agreement between them.) This new doctrine in the law exists only in some states.

Child custody: John and Mary will have the rights and duties of care and control of their child following a divorce or separation. Legal custody is the right and duty to make vital decisions about the child's education, medical care, religious training, and similar issues. There are two basic arrangements:

1. Custody in one parent with visitation rights in the other

    Usually, the child lives with one parent (the custodial parent) while the noncustodial parent may visit with the child.

2. Joint custody

    John and Mary both have legal custody. The child may live with each of them at different times.

    The court usually decides *contested* custody cases on a standard of the "best interest of the child." As you can imagine, this is often a difficult standard to apply. The court considers such factors as the past history of child care, the fitness of the parent(s), and, in some cases, the child's wishes.

Child support: Payment for the child's care and support from the noncustodial parent to the custodial parent. These payments usually end at the child's *age of majority,* or when he completes his education, or when he becomes *emancipated*. (See **Who Is a Person?**, page 16.)

Division of property: What property do John and Mary get after a divorce? Property includes anything that can be owned, such as a house, land, jewelry, money, stocks, patents, and rights (e.g., a copyright on a book).

There are two major division patterns in the different states. . . .

1. Common law (separate property):

   John and Mary may each have their own property (separate property) and may hold property together, such as a car or a house (marital property).

   In a divorce they (or the court) decide how to divide all the different categories of property, according to *equitable distribution*. (See **Law and Equity**, page 6.)

2. Community property

   John and Mary generally continue to hold what they had before the marriage. However, all property earned during the marriage is owned by both (community property).

   In a divorce this community property is divided equally between them. The premarriage property generally remains with John or Mary, as it was.

Divorce decree: The *court order* that ends the marriage. It determines all the issues between John and Mary.

Interlocutory decree (decree nisi): A temporary decree, issued during the proceedings. There is generally a waiting period before the decree can become final.

Final decree: Issued at the end of all proceedings. Any breach of the decree is treated as *contempt of court*.

WILLS

The language of the who, what, where, when, why, and how of wills.

WHO

Who are the players? Note: Some terms have a masculine and feminine form:

MALE	FEMALE
testator	testatrix
administrator	administratrix
executor	executrix
heir	heiress

Testator, testatrix: The person making the will.
Decedent: A person who has died.

The people inheriting property under a will or through intestacy (see page 59) are called by various terms:

Beneficiary: A person or organization entitled to receive property from a will (or from a trust or insurance policy).

Heir, heiress: A person or institution who will inherit—either because he is named in the will or because he is entitled to inherit from the decedent by law.

Issue: Descendants, children, grandchildren, et cetera.

Next of kin: The people closest to the decedent in blood relationship. Also, people who will receive property because of their relationship (under the laws of intestacy).

The people who have various functions under a will or through intestacy include the following:

Administrator/administratrix: Someone named by a court to manage the estate of a decedent who dies without leaving a will.

Custodian: A general term. Anyone who has charge (custody) of property, papers, or persons (such as minor children). Sometimes called a conservator.

Executor/executrix: A person named in a will to manage the decedent's estate. Also called a personal representative.

Guardian: A person named in the will or by the court to care for a minor child or a person who has been decreed by a court to be not competent to care for himself. Sometimes also manages property.

These persons serve with or without bond.

Bond: A guarantee to pay money to persons damaged or hurt by the failure of the person in position of trust, such as a trustee, executor, administrator, or guardian, to carry out his legal and ethical duty. Bonds are written by bonding or surety companies. Their cost is based on the value of the estate.

WHAT

Will: The document, signed by the testator and witnessed according to law where the testator is domiciled, which explains how he wishes to have property distributed after death, who should care for minor children, et cetera. To be valid a will must be written and executed (signed/witnessed/completed) according to the law of the testator's domicile. (See page 57.) Also called the last will and testament, if you care to get fancy!

Estate: All property—real and personal—that a person owns when he dies.

Gift: Property given in a will. There are two types of gifts:

1. Devise: Real property; that is, real estate, including land, house, the barn by the old mill stream. It includes whatever is attached to the land.

2. Legacy or bequest: Personal property. All property other than land, including money, cars, paintings, insurance policies, jewelry, et cetera.

Thus, the furnace is a devise; but the space heater is a bequest or legacy.

Dower and curtesy: The common law right (by state or common law) that a surviving spouse has to receive or enjoy and use real property. This is the right to a "life estate." The spouse gets (or has the right to use for life) a portion of the decedent's estate if provisions were not made in the will or if the survivor chooses to take or elect against the will. (See below.)

Dower refers to the widow's right; *curtesy* to the widower's. Lovely old terms, aren't they? These rights have been abolished or changed in most states.

Elect against the will: All states allow a surviving spouse to ignore the provisions made for him in the will (if any) and choose instead the financial allocation provided in the state's statutes. Usually, these give him one half or one third of the estate.

Inherit: To receive property from a decedent either through a will or through intestacy.

Disinherit: A testator can intentionally omit a legal heir who would normally have a right to inherit, such as a child. Children can be disinherited in most states, but spouses cannot. (See **elect against the will,** page 56.)

Legacy: general, specific, and residuary gifts of personal property (bequests) in a will.

A general legacy gives a specified amount of money, but its source is unspecified. "I give one thousand dollars to Andrew."

A specific legacy gives a designated property. "I give the antique diamond to Kate"; or "all stock in Corporation X to Kenneth"; or "all moneys in First National Bank to Aaron."

A residuary legacy is all the bequests remaining after other legacies have been distributed. "I give all that remains to Jonah."

WHERE

Domicile: The place where a person has his principal home.

The will is probated where the person lived when he died. That's where the will is written.

WHEN

There are two relevant time periods: before death and after death.

1. Before death

Mental capacity: The will is written when the testator is of "sound mind"; that is, he knows what document he is signing and what he is giving away. His decisions are made without fraud or undue influence from someone who may inherit from him.

All wills are revocable and changeable before the testator's death. He may add to a will as often as he wishes, since a will does not become effective until death. However, all changes must be made by following the proper procedures. Again, check local law.

Codicil: An amendment to a will. It is a separate legal document that changes an existing will and must be signed and witnessed just like the original will.

Revocation: The cancellation of an instrument, such as a will, before it becomes effective.

2. After death

Probate: Establishing the validity of the will, either by witnesses or by a self-proving will. Also, probate is the process by which an executor or administrator is appointed, estate taxes and debts are paid, the estate is collected, heirs are identified, and, finally, the estate is distributed.

Proving a will: A legal action to determine if a will is valid and authentic and may be probated. Also may be called a "will contest."

Self-proving will: A will that avoids the above contest. This is done by having witnesses, at the time the will is written, sign affidavits before a notary attesting to the fact that they witnessed the will signing. On this matter, as on all others in the field, each state has its own very specific statutes that must be followed.

Common ways to avoid property going through probate: placing property in joint tenancy, giving gifts before death, and creating trusts. This book does not detail these terms.

WHY

You write a will in order to be testate: to die with a valid will. In this way the testator/testatrix decides how the estate is to be distributed. Otherwise you die intestate.

To be intestate: To die without a valid will. In case of intestacy the estate is distributed according to state law, generally to close family members, next of kin. A guardian for young children is appointed by state officials.

A sample common order of intestacy:

> spouse
> children
> parents
> siblings
> nieces and nephews
> other next of kin

Escheat: If a person dies without a will and has no relatives who qualify to inherit, the property escheats to the state. It goes to the state! It does not go to a lifelong companion or best friend or favorite charity. Doesn't this word sounds like what it means!

Death tax, inheritance tax, transfer tax, estate tax: All mean approximately the same thing—a tax levied by state and federal governments on the decedent's property, above a certain amount. For example, after 1987 the federal estate tax exemption is six hundred thousand dollars. That is, no taxes are paid on the first six hundred thousand dollars of an estate. Taxes and exemption amounts differ from state to state, of course.

HOW

Intent: A very important legal concept in this area of the law as well as many others. (See **When What Is in Your Heart and Mind Does Matter,** page 108). If a will dispute develops, the court will attempt to determine the decedent's intention at the time he wrote the will in order to carry out those wishes. The critical question will be: What did the decedent intend to do? As you can imagine, this is not easy to determine if a will is ambiguous.

INDIVIDUAL INCOME TAXES

Income-tax procedures are complex, even after Congress's recent revisions of the Internal Revenue Code in the name of "tax simplification."

The least a taxpayer can do is learn the language! So, here goes. . . .

Internal Revenue Code (IRC): The statutes dealing with federal tax law. These include income, estate, gift, excise, and stamp taxes. For the IRC look in Title 26 of the United States Code (USC). Happy reading! It's several thousand pages long—of very fine print!

Tax: A compulsory assessment of a person, corporation, trust, or other taxable entity and property for money to support the government. It is *not* a voluntary contribution!

Income: All the moneys you make, including salaries, tips, profits, interest and dividends, lottery prize winnings, commissions, royalties, alimony received, capital gains, rents, gains from the sale of real estate, and everything else! It's all the money you make in your business, your work, and your investments.

You make it, the government gets a piece of it! But it wasn't always so. Before 1913 an income tax was unconstitutional. Then the Sixteenth Amendment was ratified, which gave Congress the right to tax income "from whatever source derived."

Tax return: The document a taxpayer provides to the Internal Revenue Service, detailing his income and tax liability.

Internal Revenue Service (IRS): The federal agency that administers the IRC. It is part of the Treasury Department.

1040 form: This form, mailed to all taxpayers who filed in the past, provides forms and instructions. . . . It comes around January first of every year. It's a New Year's present we all get!

Here are the basic terms:

Gross income: The total money you bring in from all sources. (See page 60.) In divorce it includes alimony received but not lump-sum payments or child support. It includes valuables you find, but not gifts you get. (The donor may be taxed on gifts to an individual over ten thousand dollars per year. Gift tax is not dealt with here.) It does get complex!

Gross income is the biggest sum that appears on your tax return. Luckily, everyone gets to subtract (deduct) from that—bit by bit—to get to the all-important *bottom line,* the actual taxable income. (It's from your taxable income that you compute the taxes you owe, based on various formulae and charts. . . . But we have a long way to go before we get to that!) So, here we go. . . .

Adjustments to income: These are deductions you can take for various purposes, such as tax-deferred retirement accounts (IRAs), self-employment health insurance deductions (above a specified amount), reimbursed employee business expenses, and alimony (but not child support) you paid to your ex-spouse. (This list is not totally inclusive; there may be other adjustments.)

Total adjustments: All the deductions you can take as adjustments to income.

Adjusted gross income: Your gross income minus the adjustments.

Deductions: Amounts you can deduct from your adjusted gross income. You can do this in two ways:

1. Use the standard deduction: For 1989 taxes this amount was $5,200 for a joint return filed by a married couple with dependent child. Note, of course, that 1989 taxes are paid in 1990.

2. Use itemized deductions: You can deduct various expenses. For example, certain expenses are deductible dollar for dollar: state and local income and real estate taxes, charitable gifts, mortgage interest, moving expenses, et cetera. Other expenses are deductible above a certain amount, such as medical and dental expenses, casualty losses and thefts, unreimbursed employee business expenses, tax preparation expenses, and so on. These lists are not all-inclusive; there may be other items. This is where you need all those stubs and careful notes you take all year. If you deduct an expense, you may have to be able to prove that you paid it.

Obviously, in choosing between the standard or itemized deduction route, you use whichever gives you the larger deduction (that you can prove).

We move on. . . .

Exemption: An additional amount you can deduct, depending on the number of dependents you have. You get an exemption for yourself, for your spouse, and for each dependent. The value of an exemption has changed over the years. It's now around two thousand dollars.

Taxable income (also called **Net Income**): The amount of income left after figuring in adjustments and deductions.

Compute the tax: Take your taxable income and decide how much tax you owe, based on your filing status: Are you single? married? filing a joint return with your spouse or married and filing separately? an individual return? as a head of household?

These all lead to different tax rates, which appear in the tax tables. Most favorable is a married, joint return.

Credits: An amount subtracted from the tax. Credits are now allowed for such items as child and dependent care, elderly and disabled care, and foreign tax credit. Again, this list is not all-inclusive.

Now, unfortunately, you may have to add to the tax owed.

Other taxes: Taxes including self-employment taxes, Social Security taxes on tip income not reported, and others.

Total tax: The Bottom Line, at last! This is the tax owed. You subtract what has been withheld by your employer (shown on the W-2 form) and what you paid during the year at this time. . . .

If you paid more than you owe, you get a refund. If you owe more than you paid, you owe the difference.

"I owe, I owe, it's off to work I go." And the cycle begins anew!

OTHER TERMS

Income is divided into capital gains and ordinary income.

Ordinary income: All income that does not qualify as capital gains income.

Capital gains income: Money made on the sale or exchange of capital assets. These include your home, stocks and bonds, et cetera. Anything you sell, excluding what you usually sell to your customers.

Capital gains are further separated into short-term gains (or losses) and long-term capital gains (or losses).

Long term is for something held for more than twelve months; short term is for something held less than twelve months. Over the years Congress has changed the way both of these are taxed. By doing that Congress is engaged in both revenue collection and social planning. Which of these gains gets favorable treatment? What policies are encouraged? Is it investments? savings? growth? In 1989 long- and short-term gains were taxed at the same rate as ordinary income. In earlier years long-term gains were taxed at lower rates. It's a fascinating process to watch!

Filing status: Whether you file as a single person, married person with a joint return, married person filing separately, or head of household. Each status has its own reasons and advantages.

Head of household: An unmarried taxpayer who maintains a household with at least one dependent and satisfies certain criteria established by the IRS. This, too, is an area of flux, as Congress grapples with the changing criteria in society.

Why does someone want to be considered a head of household instead of a single person? To qualify for the favorable tax rates, of course.

Graduated tax: Tax system in which the tax rate increases with the taxpayer's income. The income tax system is a graduated tax. For example, in 1989, a married taxpayer filing jointly paid fifteen percent on the first $30,950 of taxable income; twenty-eight percent on income between $30,950 and $74,850; thirty-three percent on income between $74,850 and $155,320; a lower percentage, depending on circumstances, on taxable income over $155,320. Note how the percentages increase as income increases, up to $155,320.

Progressive tax: Another term for the graduated tax. The social policy goal is to tax the wealthy proportionally more than the poor.

Regressive tax: The opposite of a progressive tax. Here, the tax rate increases less than the income base. Thus, it falls more heavily on poorer taxpayers.

April fifteenth: Midnight! Tax returns are due. Taxes are due. A good time to get a temporary job at the IRS!

Automatic extension: Tax returns are normally due on April fifteenth. You are entitled to extend that time by four months (until August fifteenth) by filing a form *and* paying your taxes (as you estimate them) by April fifteenth. If your estimates are too low, you will pay the penalties discussed below. The automatic extension does not change the deadline for payment of taxes due.

There are several ways to get in trouble with the IRS. Including:

Failure to file a tax return: If you fail to file a return, you may be charged a penalty for not (or late) filing, the taxes owed plus interest, and a penalty for late payment of taxes.

Failure to pay taxes: If you file a return but fail to pay taxes, you may be charged a penalty, along with the taxes owed.

Underpayment of taxes: If you pay less tax than you owe, you may be charged interest, compounded daily, on all that you owe. The rate is adjusted twice a year and based on the prime rate. It used to be clever to "borrow" from Uncle Sam because the back interest rates were low. Alas, they no longer are.

Underpayment of taxes because of overvaluation of property: If you pay less tax than you owe because you overvalued your property, you will pay a penalty depending on how much you overvalued the property—for example, if you exaggerated a charitable deduction or the basis of (i.e., what you paid for) a capital asset.

Understatement of tax liability: If you substantially understate the tax you owe, you may be penalized.

Negligence penalties: If your underpayment is caused by negligence, you may pay a penalty.

Fraud penalties: If your underpayment is caused by fraud, you may pay a hefty penalty, and often criminal penalties.

Criminal penalties: If you ''willfully'' evade or cheat the tax law, penalties include fines, imprisonment for up to five years, or both.

Tax avoidance and tax evasion: They are not the same thing. Tax avoidance is legal. It's the tax planning you may do to pay the minimum tax legally.

Tax evasion is illegal. It is the intentional payment of less tax than is due, by use of fraud, false statements, false records, et cetera. Basically, it is filing a false tax return. It is a crime.

Statute of limitations: The IRS is given three years from the time you file your return to audit you. If you don't file a return, they may come after you anytime, as the statute of limitation does not begin to run until you do so.

If you file a return but omit items that amount to more than twenty-five percent of your gross income, the IRS has six years to come after you!

If you commit tax fraud, the IRS can come after you anytime. It has no time limits.

Audit: An examination of a taxpayer's financial records by an IRS agent.

There are several levels:

A correspondence audit is done through the mails. The IRS asks for information and the taxpayer mails it in.

An office audit is conducted in the IRS agent's office.

A field audit is conducted at the place of business or home of the taxpayer.

Appeal: If you dispute the results of the audit, you may appeal them to the supervisor, the IRS administrative hearing, or Tax Court or other federal court.

Tax Court: The Tax Court of the United States has jurisdiction over cases in which the IRS and taxpayers dispute the amount of taxes owed.

To get into this court the IRS has to issue a statutory Notice of Deficiency (called ''the ninety-day letter'') and the taxpayer has to file a petition for a hearing within the specified time.

OTHER TERMS ABOUT TAXES: NOT INCOME

Estate tax: Tax on the transfer of property at death. Called a ''transfer tax'' in some states. (See page 59.)

Inheritance tax: Tax on the right to receive property. This exists only in a few states.

Gift tax: A federal tax on a donor's gift if it amounts to more than ten thousand dollars per year to any individual. Some states tax the donee. There is also a lifetime exemption providing no taxes below the exempt amount.

Tax lien: The government's claim on a property as security for taxes due. Yes, they can force you to sell your property to collect the taxes.

And there you have it. The key tax terms in twelve pages or less!

MALPRACTICE

Malpractice is a combination of tort and **K** laws. Cases deal with all types of professionals: doctors, lawyers, engineers, architects, stockbrokers, and so on. (See torts at page 27. See contracts at page 39.)

Dr. Smith operated on Mr. Jones to improve a persistent backache. Jones's condition worsened. . . .

Jones now wonders whether Dr. Smith's treatment constitutes malpractice. To find out he should ask the following questions:

1. Duty of Due Care

ASK: Did Dr. Smith have a duty to care for Mr. Jones reasonably? with due care?

This *duty of due care* exists in most patient/doctor situations. But, at an accident site, for example, if Dr. Smith stops to give assistance to Jones (not his patient), he cannot be sued for malpractice in most states. He is protected by the *Good Samaritan doctrine,* which limits suits against doctors to cases of *gross negligence.*

IF THERE WAS DUTY OF CARE . . . GO TO NEXT STEP.

IF NOT . . . STOP. (There is no malpractice.)

2. Breach of Duty

ASK: Did Dr. Smith fail to practice medicine as other doctors in his specialty do?

or

Was his conduct below the standard of his profession?

or

Did he fail to get the necessary "informed consent" before the treatment?

Dr. Smith has a duty to practice medicine according to the standards of his profession, as other doctors in his specialty do, and to treat patients according to the scope of their informed consent.

If Jones is unsatisfied with the treatment results, malpractice is not necessarily involved. Dr. Smith may have practiced standard medicine. No tort may have been committed. Jones might be able to sue on a *contract* theory: if the results were less than promised.

IF THERE WAS A BREACH OF DUTY . . . GO TO NEXT STEP.

IF NOT . . . STOP. (There is no malpractice.)

3. Causation

ASK: Did Dr. Smith *cause* Mr. Jones's harm? (Remember, this is a *tort* question. See page 28.)

If Dr. Smith misdiagnosed Jones's condition and treated it wrong, AND if Jones could have improved with the right treatment, Dr. Smith may have *caused* the harm.

If, on the other hand, Jones's condition was untreatable, then the "wrong" treatment did not *cause* the harm. It may have happened anyway.

If a patient claims he did not give an "informed consent" to treatment, he must also prove that he would have declined treatment if he'd had more information. If it is proven that he would have consented even with additional information, then the lack of an "informed consent" did not cause the harm.

IF THERE WAS CAUSATION . . . GO TO NEXT STEP.

IF NOT . . . STOP. (There is no malpractice.)

4. The Doctor's Defenses

ASK: Does Dr. Smith have any valid defenses?

For example, the Good Samaritan doctrine, the *immunity* of government doctors, and the emergency situation when the doctor does not have the time to get an "informed consent." (See page 109.)

IF THERE ARE VALID DEFENSES . . . THERE MAY NOT BE MALPRACTICE.

IF THERE ARE NO VALID DEFENSES . . . THERE MAY BE A MALPRACTICE CLAIM.

THE AMAZING LIFE OF A CHECK

Why is it called a check when it's actually a bill?

A check is an order by one person (the drawer) that a second person (the drawee, usually a bank) pay a sum of money to a third person (the payee). Got that?

A check can be written on any piece of paper and is valid as long as the following conditions are met:

1. It states "pay to the order of . . ."
2. It states a definite amount of money.
3. It's signed by the drawer.
4. It states the drawee's name.

To draw a check is to write a check.

The drawer writes the check to the order of the payee. The drawer is liable for the money. Know your drawer! This is why stores are often reluctant to take checks from customers they do not know. If it's a bad check and they endorse it, they may be stuck with no payment and liable for that check. Once the payee receives the check, he makes presentment for payment by signing his name on (endorsing) the back of the check. The payee's endorsement on the back in effect *transfers* the check into a new contract. Now the payee/endorser may be liable for the check.

If the endorser turns the check over to another

person but does not want to guarantee payment, he writes, ''Without recourse,'' above his signature on the back of the check.

If he (the payee/endorser) seeks to limit his liability, he can limit the endorsement. A common way is to write, ''For deposit only, Account # XYXY,'' when he makes his presentment.

What happens to a check once it leaves the payee/endorser? It travels (physically or electronically) to the drawer's bank for collection from the drawer's account at the drawee bank.

Here are some possible adventures on the way:

1. The check *clears*. This means there is enough money in the drawer's account to cover it. Nice and easy.

2. The check *bounces*. This is called a bad check or a rubber check (because it bounces back to the payee). There is not enough money in the drawer's account to cover it. Bad news. The drawee dishonors the check, sending it back with a statement ''Returned for insufficient funds.''

3. Overdraft: If the drawer's account does not have enough money, the drawee may cover for it and charge the drawer for that service. In this case the drawer is borrowing from the drawee.

4. Larceny by False Pretenses: Things can get worse. If the drawer knowingly writes a bad check, this is a fraudulent criminal offense. It may be called ''larceny by false pretense.''

5. Forgery: The unauthorized signing of your name or altering the dollar amount of the check. If the forgery is in writing your name as drawer, the forgery will not transfer the funds out of your account, so long as you inform your bank of the forgery in a ''timely fashion,'' that is, SOON. If, however, you endorse a forged check, you may be liable. (See the example of the storekeepers above.)

6. Stale check: If a check is older than six months, the bank may not honor it.

REAL ESTATE: THE LAW OF HOME SWEET HOME

Real estate refers to buying and selling a house. Real estate also refers to realty: land, houses, trees, driveway, barn, and everything else attached to the land. Everything else is personal property, or personalty: cars, jewelry, furniture, lawn mower.

Sally and Sam Sellers want to sell their house. When they do, they'll be the grantors. As you'll see, this is quite a process.

First they have to answer some basic questions.

How do they hold title? That is, what do they own that they can sell?

TYPE OF TITLE HELD BY SELLER

Fee: Ownership of real estate. Funny word. Comes from fiefdom in the Middle Ages.

There are various types of ownership interests. For example:

Fee simple, or fee simple absolute: Complete ownership, with the right to sell or devise (give in a will) the property.

"I grant, sell, convey my house at ——— to William Smith *and his heirs and assigns forever.*"

Most American homeowners have this type of fee.

Fee simple conditional: Complete ownership, but limited in some way. For example, property sold (devised) so long as it's used for religious purposes; or as a farm; or whatever. If ever the use changes, then the property reverts (goes back) to the grantor or his heirs or assigns. This is called a "reversion."

"I grant, sell, convey my house at ——— to Brother John *so long as it is used for religious purposes.*"

If you buy or get one of these properties, you'd better know about this condition!

Life estate: Freehold interest with no inheritance rights. Ownership for the life of the person holding it or some other life (*per autre vie*). When the person dies, the life estate terminates and the fee simple reverts to the grantor or his heirs.

"I grant, sell, convey my house at ——— to Kate Brown as long as she lives or as long as ——— lives (the other life; the *autre vie*)."

Two other forms of ownership are new; created by statute—not the old common law. As you can see, these are hybrids of the law: part this and part that! These are:

1. Condominium: The owner has separate ownership of an airspace inside an individual apartment, office space, et cetera, in a multiple-unit building or complex of buildings. The owner also has a right to use (and part ownership of) the common areas, such as the halls, elevators, land, walls, garage, swimming pool, whatever.

The single unit is a fee simple; the shared areas are tenancies in common. (See below.)

2. Cooperative: The entire property—real estate (land, buildings) and personal property related to it (lawn mowers, snowblowers, shovels) is owned by a cooperative corporation. Every "owner" owns a share of stock in the corporation and is entitled to a "proprietary lease" from the corporation of a unit—a dwelling, office, et cetera. The corporation may have a loan from a bank used to buy the property. If so, if one member defaults in his payments, all members chip in to cover the default. Often an owner will get a personal loan from a bank to buy his or her share of stock. This is an individual—not group—obligation.

Let's assume Sally and Sam have a fee simple absolute.

TYPE OF OWNERSHIP INTEREST

Next, how do they hold it? What does each of them actually own that each can sell? As you may have guessed, there are several forms of ownership. These include, among others, the following:

Sole tenancy; also called several tenancy or tenancy in severalty: One person owns the entire property and can sell it or devise it (unless he's getting a divorce in a community property state and acquired the property during the marriage). (See **community property,** below.)

Joint tenancy with right of survivorship: Two persons own the entire property in equal interests. If one dies, the property goes to the other. The conveyance must clearly state the intent to form this tenancy: "To Sally and Sam as joint tenants *with the right of survivorship.*"

Tenancy by the entirety with right of survivorship: A special form of joint tenancy, only possible for married couples.

Tenancy in common: Property held by two or more persons, each owning a separate and separable interest, with no right of survivorship. When an owner dies, his interest is devised to his heirs, not to his cotenant. This can make for strange bedfellows!

Community property: (Exists only in some states.) Property obtained after the marriage, through the work and efforts of one or both spouses, becomes the property of both, regardless of how the title is held. (See **sole tenancy,** page 75.) In case of divorce the property is divided equally. At death, however, the decedent's interest passes to his heirs; the survivor retains his interest.

In legalese, this is because there is no automatic right of survivorship to the spouse in community property.

Let's assume Sally and Sam own the property as tenants by the entirety and can sell it.

REAL ESTATE BROKER

Next, they decide whether to sell the house on their own or with a real estate broker (or "agent" or "realtor." For our purposes these professionals are treated interchangeably).

Let's assume they opt to use a broker. The broker is the seller's representative (agent). Therefore, when the house sells, it's the seller/grantor who will pay the commission. Buyers beware!

Commission: A fee paid to the broker for services performed. It's not a salary, which generally is payment for time worked. A commission is usually the same amount whether it takes one week or one year to find a buyer. The amount of the fee is usually a percentage of the sale price.

Sally, Sam, and the broker enter into a listing agreement—yes, another contract (**K**)! Sally and Sam will agree to pay a commission if the broker sells the house (and sometimes even if he doesn't. Watch this one!).

As you probably guessed, there are several types of listing agreements. For example:

1. Exclusive: Here, the broker gets a commission if the house is sold during the period of the agency, no matter who sells it! Thus, even if you alone find someone to buy it, you owe the commission.

To avoid this, when writing the listing agreement (**K**), the seller may be able to write in an exception for the potential buyers who have already been shown the house. Then, if any of them buy it, there will be no commission.

2. Open listing: You can list your house with any and all agents you wish. Whoever sells it gets the commission. It's a free-for-all.

3. Multiple listing service (MLS): Here, you list your house with a broker, who places it on a master list to which all member brokers have access. Your broker is the "listing broker." Then the broker who sells your house splits the commission with the listing broker.

When does a broker get paid? There are lots of different possible times: when the house is sold at closing; or when he or she presents a buyer who is "ready, willing, and able" to buy your house; or when you reach a purchase and sale agreement; or . . .

Make sure you get the listing agreement to say what you want. Negotiate and read carefully before you sign!

Yeah! Just when you were tired of cleaning your house all the time and had given up hope of selling it . . . here come Betsy and Bill Buyer. They love your house! They are "ready, willing, and able" to buy it.

If they actually buy the house, they will be the grantees. Great! Break out the champagne? No, not quite so fast. . . .

It's time to write a purchase and sale agreement (P & S). (Again, a K!)

THE PURCHASE AND SALE AGREEMENT

What's in a purchase and sale agreement? It should state all the important terms of the agreement between the buyer and seller, such as the price, date, and other important terms. Who gets the carpeting? the stove? the chandelier? and so on. It may include the following legalistic terms:

1. Date: The date for transfer of the house (the actual sale) is listed in the P & S agreement. If the date is critical to either party, it should state, "Time is of the essence." If not, the date may be changed without penalty or breach of K.

2. Title: What type of ownership can the seller convey? Not all owners own the same rights even if they "own" their own house.

The seller's ownership (title) can be affected (limited) by an:

Encumbrance: Any right someone has to the property, such as a lien, lease, mortgage, easement, taxes due, et cetera.

Lien: A legal claim against the property. For example, a tax lien for taxes owed, a mechanic's lien for payment for work performed on the property, a judgment lien for payment of a court order. There are lots of types of liens.

Mortgage: (See financing, page 80.)

Easement: A right others have to use your property for specific purposes. For example, someone may have a right to cross it to get to a road; a utility company may have rights to construct and repair power lines on it. Easements are created either in writing or through continued use. "But we've always gone this way. Now you can't stop us. We have an easement!" Or "We've always parked here." Well, you get the idea.

Covenants that "run with the land." A covenant is an agreement. One that "runs with the land" "touches and concerns" the land. For example, there may be "no liquor" laws; there may be restrictions in the subdivision. These covenants must be in writing.

Zoning regulations: These are governmental rules and restrictions that regulate the types or use of buildings and land. They may be ordinances and bylaws. For example, in a historic district the renovations you make may be restricted. In a residential area you may not be able to have your office at home, with clients coming and going. In a commercial district you will undoubtedly have to build according to codes and standards.

Riparian rights: Rights belonging to the owners on the banks of a river (sometimes a sea or lake also). These give all owners along the river the right to use it for useful purposes, as long as they don't deprive others of use of the water.

Lease: An agreement that sets up a landlord-tenant relationship on the land. Unless the lease says otherwise, even if you sell the property, you may not be able to evict the tenant until the end of the lease period.

The buyer/grantee gets title insurance. The insurance protects the buyer against any deficiencies ("clouds") in the title.

Other terms in a P & S agreement:

Financing: The buyer who does not have enough cash to pay the entire price for the home (as most of us don't), will seek a mortgage.

A mortgage is a written document, in which the borrower (mortgagor) pledges his property as security in exchange for getting a loan from the mortgagee (often, a bank). The property is the mortgagee's security interest. The mortgage is a conditional transfer of legal title pending repayment of the loan. The mortgagee retains the right to redeem legal title in case the mortgagor defaults.

If all goes well, after a specific period of time of paying mortgage payments (for example, fifteen years or thirty years), the legal title to the house will again belong to the grantee/buyer and he can "burn" the mortgage.

If all does not go so well, particularly if he fails to make his payments (he defaults), the mortgagee may foreclose the mortgagor's right to redeem legal title to the house. The mortgagor may be forced out and the house may be sold at a foreclosure sale.

But let's not worry about this now. . . .

Inspection: The grantee/buyer will seek to have the property inspected by an engineer and termite inspector.

Let's assume all goes well—you get a mortgage, there are no termites, the house will stand for the next hundred years—no problem! It's on to the closing!

THE CLOSING AND THE DEED

Closing: The transfer of title from grantor to grantee (seller to buyer) by a deed. Basically, the buyer pays for the house at the closing.

Deed: A signed document that transfers property. The transfer is also called a "conveyance."

Again, have you guessed? There are several types of deeds, depending on how much is promised and sold.

Remember that a covenant is an agreement, a **K**. A warranty is a promise that the title is good. The buyer may be buying one of several types:

Full covenant and warranty deed: The best! It conveys good title to the property, that it is free of any encumbrances. The grantee/buyer gets a covenant of quiet enjoyment. Lovely term, isn't it? It means that no one can have competing claims or better title to his property. *Quiet* here means that no one can disturb your right of ownership. Yes, he might still be bothered by loud parties or dogs. That gets into another area of law altogether— nuisance in tort law! (See above at page 36.)

Bargain and sale deed: Not so good. This covenant does not guarantee title. Here, the grantor/seller warrants that he has not done or will not do anything to interfere with the grantee's quiet enjoyment. But there may be a prior defect in the title. No promises (warranties) are made about that.

Quitclaim deed: Here, the grantee buys "as is." The grantor conveys all he has but makes no warranties about what that might be. In some states he also warrants that he did not impair the title.

Title insurance protects against encumbrances you don't know about, such as survey errors.

Other provisions in a deed:

Consideration: As in any K the deed will list the amount paid.

Legal description of the property: Description of the exact boundaries of the property measured in longitude and latitude (degrees and minutes) or metes and bounds (listing distances of the boundaries; using compass directions).

Granting language: The words of transfer. "I, Miriam Freedman, sell my house to Paul Harris and his heirs and assigns forever. . . ."

Habendum clause: It starts with words "To have and to hold. . . ." It usually follows the granting clause. (See above.)

Signatures: Signing the deed authenticates it; says you mean to do what the deed says.

Notary: Is proof that the document has been executed (signed, completed, et cetera); that it was a free act by the parties. Sometimes a seal is used. Sometimes the notary's jurat is sufficient: stating the date, location, and person before whom the deed is signed. As in "Signed, sealed, and delivered"!)

Recording: The deed should be filed at the local recording office or registrar of deeds (usually the courthouse).

Why would you want to do this? So that the entire world has notice of your deed. It creates a record of ownership. Mortgages and liens are also recorded to give notice that the property is thus encumbered.

The type of notice created here is called "constructive notice." *Constructive* means "as if." This means that anyone who may make a claim against the property is deemed to have been notified of its status, whether or not he or she actually went to the records to check. That person can't claim he didn't know about the sale or the mortgage or lien, or whatever. He had notice and should have known.

Now—finally—congratulations. Break out the champagne! Betsy and Bill Buyer, you are homeowners!

LANDLORD AND TENANT LAW

Landlord-tenant law varies from state to state and city to city. So beware! This is also a fast-changing area of the law. Here are some of the terms you'll need to know.

BEFORE THE TENANCY

Lease: A lease is an agreement between the landlord and tenant. The landlord gives up *possession* of the property in exchange for the payment of rent by the tenant. The tenant gets *possession* of the premises. Note that the landlord keeps the ownership of the property. Possession is the right to use the property for the term of the lease only. Other terms for leasing property include . . . *to let, to rent, to demise.*

1. The parties
Lessor is the landlord.
Lessee is the tenant.

The lease may include these words: **"Joint and several liability."** If more than one tenant signs the lease, each is responsible for the entire amount of rent. Thus, if one tenant fails to pay his share, the lessor can seek payment from the other tenant for the entire amount.

2. Leased property: The land and/or building(s) which are the subject of the lease.

3. Term: Specifies the amount of time the property is leased. Several types of leases include:

Periodic tenancy: Also called "tenancy for years" (though it may be for weeks or months). This form of tenancy continues from month to month or week to week, whatever its terms. Generally it is automatically renewed for the same time period unless the lessor or lessee gives notice that it should end when that period ends.

Tenancy for years: This form of tenancy is for a specific time period. It is not automatically renewed. When the lease is up, the lessee is supposed to move out (vacate the premises) without any action by either the lessor or the lessee. That is, notice is generally not required. Of course, the parties may agree to enter into a new lease.

Tenancy at will: This tenancy is for an undetermined time period. It can end by either lessor or lessee notifying the other. Note that in many states the landlord is required to give the tenant a thirty-day *notice*. Thus the *tenant at will* is, in actuality, a *periodic tenant* for thirty days! (See above.)

ALSO, **Tenancy at sufferance:** If a tenant remains on the property after his tenancy without the landlord's *consent,* he becomes a "holdover tenant," a tenant at sufferance.

4. Rent . . . is rent. Usually, money. The lessee's payment for the right to occupy the premises. Rents may also include expenses for taxes, utilities (heat and light), and other necessities.

DURING THE TENANCY

Certain warranties or covenants may apply.

Warranty: An assurance by one *party* that certain facts exist on which the other party can rely.

Covenant: A written agreement that specifies promises and obligations.

Some examples:

Warrant (or Covenant) of Quiet Enjoyment: The lessor provides the lessee with the right of unimpaired use and enjoyment of the premises. This means that no one with a better *title* to the property than the landlord has will disturb the lease. For example, if a building is sold during the tenancy, and the tenant is ordered to move out, that would breach this warranty. No, this warranty is not for a quiet place (without noise!) unless the noise or other nuisance (a **tort,** see page 27) is so bad that the premises become uninhabitable.

Warrant (or Covenant) of Habitability: Promises that there are no latent, or hidden, defects in the premises that would make it unfit for use. If warranties are breached, some possible remedies by lessees in different jurisdictions include the following. (Check local laws! These differ greatly from jurisdiction to jurisdiction.)

Abatement: A decrease, reduction. Paying less than the full amount of rent.

Repair and deduct: The tenant repairs the defects in the premises (which he had reported to the landlord) and deducts the repair cost from the rent.

Rent strike: A group of tenants withholds rent payments, placing the money in a special bank account (usually under court supervision), while awaiting the landlord's repair of the premises. As with the aforementioned remedies, check local laws and consult an attorney before taking any action on this, as most states limit tenant rights.

AFTER THE TENANCY

Termination: The end of the lease period. The tenant leaves the premises.

Sublet: If it's in the lease, a sublet permits the *lessee* to lease part of his interest in the property to someone else (''the sublessee''). However, if the *sublessee breaches* the lease (as in not paying rent), the *lessee* remains responsible for it.

Assignment: When the lease permits, the lessee can transfer his interest in the property to someone else (''the assignee''). In this case the assignee is primarily responsible for the rent, although the original lessor can still recover from the assignor (the original lessee) if the assignee breaches (fails to pay the rent).

Abandonment: Occurs if the tenant leaves the premises before the end of the lease without the landlord's consent. The tenant still owes the rent payments until the landlord accepts the abandonment, as in rerenting the property.

Dispossession: The tenant's losing possession of the premises, whether by legal means *(eviction)* or wrongfully (by *self-help*).

Eviction: The act of removing the tenant from the property through a court order.

Summary process: A court *procedure* that is quicker than most *civil actions* because the rights of *discovery* are limited. This is usually used in *eviction* procedures. (See **Basic Procedure in a Civil Case,** page 142.)

Self-help: When a landlord removes a tenant without court action. It is illegal.

Constructive eviction: "Constructive" is something that is not actual but is treated as if it were. Thus, *constructive eviction* occurs if the landlord does something to the property that makes it uninhabitable and that forces the tenant to leave.

Retaliatory eviction: Is illegal. It occurs when the *lessor* attempts to evict a *lessee* for asserting his rights, as in *abating* his rent, promoting a *rent strike,* etc.

AGAIN, SEE LOCAL LAW AND YOUR ATTORNEY!

REMEDIES

Once the trial is over . . .

What can courts order to enforce rights or correct injuries?

Once all witnesses and jurors go home, what then?

A menu of remedies is summarized below. Remedies are divided into three categories, based on the type of action involved: criminal, civil, and equity.

IN A CRIMINAL CASE . . .

In a criminal case a court can order:

Punishment: A fine, penalty, or confinement ordered against a defendant (Δ) by a court. The order is called a sentence. "I sentence you to . . ." (See **Punishment,** page 123.)

The Eighth Amendment of the Constitution assures us that punishment cannot be "cruel and unusual." That would be a punishment that "shocks the moral sense of the community": e.g., torture, or a disproportionate sentence—a punishment that is much too severe for the crime committed.

Confinement means loss of freedom; being held in lawful custody. Jail, prison, reformatory . . .

Fine: A pecuniary (money) punishment.

Restitution: An order for the Δ to give back what was taken, fix what was broken, and so on. Restitution is sometimes ordered as a condition of a probationary sentence.

Community service: An order that the Δ perform a job that serves a community interest, such as helping the poor, cleaning an area of a city, et cetera. Remember the actress Zsa Zsa Gabor who got seventy-two hours' worth!

IN A CIVIL CASE . . .

In a civil case a court can order:

Damages: Payment of money. The idea is to restore the parties to where they would have been if the injury or breach, et cetera, had not occurred. (See **Contracts,** page 47.)

For example, in a breach of K the plaintiff (π) may be entitled to be put in as good a position as he would have enjoyed had there been no breach. In legalese, it would "make him whole."

In torts, restitution is essentially the measure of damages. The law attempts to compensate the parties for the harm they have suffered. Of course, many cases cannot be "made whole" with money, but this is the form of remedy available in civil actions. It is as close as the law can come.

These include payments for:

Pain and suffering: The physical and mental/emotional trauma suffered by the π;

Loss of earning capacity: Attempts to measure someone's ability to earn wages in the future;

Loss of consortium: The loss of the company/love/support, et cetera, of a spouse. (See **Marriage and Divorce,** page 48.)

Over the years new forms of damages have been created by the courts.

Damages may be compensatory/actual or punitive/exemplary.

Compensatory/actual damages: Compensate the injured party for his actual injury.

Punitive/exemplary damages: Awarded to a π beyond what will compensate him, where his loss was caused by Δ's outrageous conduct, such as by fraud, malicious or willful misconduct, or intentional torts such as defamation. The damages are designed to solace the π for his mental anguish, hurt feelings, and shame, and to punish the wrongdoer. (See **Criminal and Civil Laws: What Are the Differences?,** page 9.)

Double (or treble) damages: Most often awarded in antitrust cases. The judge doubles (or triples) the jury award against a Δ, when authorized to do so by statute.

Nominal damages: A trivial amount of money to vindicate a right, where there is no real loss or injury.

Other forms of remedies:

Expectancy damages: In a breach of K these may be awarded to the π to put him back in the position he would have enjoyed if the K had been performed.

For example, you had a loan arrangement for eight percent, but the creditor breached the K. By the time you got another loan, interest rates had moved up to nine percent. You could sue for the difference, the amount of money you will lose because of the breach.

Restitution: The act of making good, of restoring, so as to prevent "unjust enrichment" by either party.

Mitigation of damages: Once there is a breach, both parties are obligated to minimize the damage. For example, if you lose a job due to a breach of K, you are obligated to seek a comparable one. You can't just sit at home waiting to collect damages. Damage awards are reduced by the amount of money that the injured party should have mitigated.

IN AN EQUITY CASE . . .

In equity cases courts have powers to grant remedies other than monetary ones. (See **Law and Equity,** page 6.) These include the following:

Injunction: A court order forbidding you from doing something you have been doing or threatening to do, or ordering you to do something. Also called a "restraining order" or an "order to cease and desist."

Injunctions and restraining orders are granted to prevent irreparable harm (harm that can't be repaired; Humpty Dumpty can't be put back). They may be used when there is no other legal means to right the *potential* wrong, when money damages may not suffice. They are designed to prevent harm, not to compensate for a past injury.

For example, your neighbor is about to cut down your tree. A husband continues to physically abuse his wife. A chemical plant dumps pollutants into the lake. Someone is infringing on your copyrighted material.

Temporary restraining order (TRO): An order forbidding someone from doing some threatened act until the matter can be heard in court. These are often issued on an emergency basis and can even be granted on an *ex parte* basis. That is, the court can grant a TRO to one party *without* prior notice to the other party. A court hearing is then scheduled to determine whether the injunction should be made permanent or lifted (ended).

Remember, these are equitable remedies—the rule of justice, safety, and necessity governs, not the rule of specific laws.

Cease and desist order: Similar to the above; designed to order a party to stop doing a harmful/forbidden act. For example, in a labor dispute one side may be ordered to stop the unfair labor practice. A union may be ordered to stop its strike and go back to work, pending mediation.

These terms, *injunction, TRO,* and *cease and desist order,* are sometimes used interchangeably.

Specific performance: In K cases. A court order to perform the K as specified. This remedy exists for cases in which monetary damages would not make the party "whole." For example, in the sale of a house, if the seller breaches the K, the buyer may seek specific performance: that is, an order forcing the seller to sell the house. The thinking behind this remedy is that since there is no house anywhere exactly like this one, specific performance is the only way to make the buyer "whole." This remedy can be ordered in the sale of goods, where the goods are unique: a *specific* painting, antique, car, and so on.

Reformation: A remedy whereby the written K between parties may be revised. This may occur because both parties made mistakes when they wrote it; or because there has been fraud. It's a way to have the K reflect the agreement actually made by the parties.

KEY CONCEPTS IN CIVIL AND CRIMINAL LAW

JURISDICTION

Being in the right place (jurisdiction) at the right time (statute of limitations) with the right stuff. (A good cause of action. In nonlegalese, a good case!)

When your lawyer tells you he's thinking about which court to use, you know it's a question of jurisdiction.

Jurisdiction is one of the most basic and important terms of American law. It is also VERY complex! This summary will introduce you to some of the main concepts. The way they work themselves out, however, is far beyond the scope of this book.

Jurisdiction is the COURT's authority to hear and decide a case. Without it you may be in the wrong place. You lose before you begin! Case dismissed for lack of JURISDICTION.

FEDERAL JURISDICTION

Generally, a *federal court* has *jurisdiction* if there is a *federal question,* or *diversity* of citizenship of parties from different states with an amount in *damages* over fifty thousand dollars.

Let's see what these terms mean.

If the plaintiff (π) is in State A and tries to sue a defendant (Δ) in State B for less than $50,000, he probably can't get Federal JURISDICTION of the Δ. He does not have Federal *in personam* jurisdiction. *(Personam =*

person.) There is no way he can summons him, notify him of the suit, compel him to appear, et cetera.

If π is in State A and trying to sue Δ in State B for more than $50,000, he can get *diversity jurisdiction* over the Δ and bring him to federal court. This jurisdiction is based on a *jurisdictional amount*. $50,000 brings you into federal court.

STATE JURISDICTION

If π is in State A and trying to sue Δ who lives (is domiciled) in State B, but who has property in State A, he may be able to gain jurisdiction over Δ's property. This is called *in rem* jurisdiction. (*Rem* = thing.)

If π is in State A and trying to sue Δ, who is in State B, he may be able to get jurisdiction through the *long-arm statutes*. These statutes are used often against national corporations as Δ's if they do business in a state, even if they are not headquartered there. This form of jurisdiction is *statutory*. (That is, it's based on a law— a *long-arm statute*.)

FEDERAL JURISDICTION

Subject matter: In general, federal courts deal with federal matters, as set out in the Constitution and later federal laws. These are called *federal questions:*

Federal questions found in the Constitution include:

    patents and trademarks and copyright
    naturalization
    admiralty
    constitutional issues
    Indian treaties

> international issues, trade, et cetera
> a citizen's suit against the federal government
> cases with diversity jurisdiction

If you get hit by a U.S. mail truck, you're in *federal court*.

And other federal questions developed since the days of the Constitution:

> federal taxes
> antitrust
> crimes across state borders, such as kidnapping
> and many more. . . .

There are special courts for many of these cases, such as Tax Court, Bankruptcy Court, Admiralty Court, Patent Court, to name just a few.

The general jurisdiction courts are the District Courts.

You must be in the right one!

STATE JURISDICTION

State courts have jurisdiction over everything else!

> marriage and divorce
> most crimes
> most contracts
> most torts
> most property cases
> most wills and trusts cases

If you get hit by any other kind of truck, you're probably in state court, unless there is diversity jurisdiction. (See page 96.) It gets complex!

Within both the federal and state court systems there are different courts for different cases. You have to be in the right one to be heard.

For example, marriage and divorce situations are probably held in Family or Probate Court. (Different names in different states.) Torts and contract cases are probably held in courts of general jurisdiction, often called District Courts, Superior Courts, or other names. Juvenile Courts deal with children, Housing Courts with houses, landlord and tenant issues, and apartments, Traffic Courts with minor traffic violations and fines, et cetera.

Each state has its own system.

CONCURRENT JURISDICTION

Sometimes someone can bring an action in either state or federal court, if there are concurrent laws—for example, in the labor/employment law area.

This is called *concurrent jurisdiction*. You choose the court where you think you have the strongest case!

Then, to really get complicated, there is also

> ancillary jurisdiction,
> pendent jurisdiction,
> original jurisdiction,
> appellate jurisdiction, among others.

Ancillary jurisdiction allows you to go to federal court with an entire complex case if that court has jurisdiction over any part of the action (even if not over all of it). This form of jurisdiction is designed to promote judicial efficiency.

Pendent jurisdiction allows you to go to federal court

if there is both a federal and state question dealing with the same event.

Original jurisdiction lies in the TRIAL COURTS. These are the first courts to which you go, where the cases are tried. The facts are decided and the law is applied.

FACTS

Facts include the following types of issues:

> Did the Δ drive through a red light?
> Was he under the influence of alcohol at the time?
> Did the Δ intend to harm the victim?
> What did the parties mean in their CONTRACT?

LAW

Law includes the following types of issues:

> What does driving under the influence signify legally?
> If the Δ intended to harm the π, does that mean he is guilty?
> Were illegal procedures used by the police?

Once a verdict or decision is reached at the trial court, the parties may, in some cases, appeal to an appellate court.

Appellate jurisdiction involves the court's power to review questions of law as they occurred at the trial court. If there were errors more than *de minimis* (insignificant), the verdict may be reversed, a new trial ordered, et cetera.

VENUE

Then, there's *venue*.

Once jurisdiction is established, a trial may be moved within that jurisdiction for the convenience of the parties or in order to assure a fair trial. This involves the principle of venue, which means the place of the trial.

A change of venue means that a trial is moved for one of the above reasons.

ADMINISTRATIVE LAW

And finally, remember that many disputes aren't handled initially in any court! They are heard by *administrative agencies*, which derive their jurisdiction from specific statutes. They are heard by officials called *hearing examiners, hearing officers,* or *administrative law judges.* . . .

For example, the Nuclear Regulatory Commission (NRC) hears cases dealing with nuclear power plants, the Federal Communications Commission (FCC) hears cases dealing with television and radio stations, licenses for them, et cetera. Social Security benefit cases are heard by the Social Security Administration (SSA).

And so it goes! Remember: Always be in the right place!

STANDARD OF PROOF

In order to prevail (win) in court, a *party* has to prove its case. PROOF IS THE NAME OF THE GAME—THE ONLY GAME IN COURT.

The *party* that brings the case to court usually has the *burden of proof* at first. In *criminal* cases this burden is always on the government. The defendant (Δ) is presumed to be innocent until proven guilty. It's the government's burden to prove him guilty. The Δ has to neither prove nor disprove anything.

In *civil suits* the plaintiff (π) has generally the first burden to present a *prima facie* case, which includes enough evidence that could prevail if not rebutted by the Δ.

What does a side need to prove its case to win? As you may have guessed by now—it depends on the case!

Beyond ALL doubt is not required in any trial.

Beyond a *reasonable* doubt is the degree to which the prosecution/government must prove its case to get a *guilty verdict* in a *criminal case*. The *jury* or *judge* (the trier of facts) must be fully satisfied with the evidence. In a jury trial there must be a unanimous verdict—all jurors must vote to convict.

Motion to dismiss may be granted by a judge when he rules (decides) that the π or prosecution has failed to meet its burden of presenting a *prima facie* case. This means that, even if everything it sought to prove is proven, it would still lose. The facts may not be determinative. The law is against the π or prosecution. (See page 99.)

By a preponderance of the evidence is the degree to which either party must prove its case to win a *civil* suit. It means that one side's evidence has greater weight than the other. A *unanimous* jury vote is generally *not* required. Each *jurisdiction* has its own standards for a necessary majority.

Note: There are cases when the government cannot *convict* a Δ, but a π in the *civil suit* on the same matter may win—because of the lower civil standard.

In a criminal case, remember that the Δ may have an affirmative defense. (See page 112.) This shifts the burden to the Δ to prove that even if he committed a criminal act, he had a valid defense, a reason, a "license," to do the act.

TIME AND ITS LEGAL CONSEQUENCES

Time is money. You can't sit on your rights forever. He who hesitates is lost. These truisms are also very important legal concepts.

Sometimes the mere passage of time will win—or lose—your case!

Two important legal concepts are based on time: The statute of limitations and retroactivity.

STATUTE OF LIMITATIONS

This time concept marches forward into the future from an event. It is a time limit on how long a person has for bringing a lawsuit or being prosecuted for a crime. Purpose: to eliminate "stale" cases. A plaintiff (π) shouldn't be rewarded for laziness or procrastination and "sitting on his rights." A defendant (Δ) shouldn't have to worry forever about being sued or prosecuted. Thus, if the time has passed, a π can lose before he ever begins his case! And, of course, a Δ can use the statute of limitations defense to move for a dismissal of the case. A motion to dismiss asks the court to throw the π's case out because it is too late; it is time barred.

Specific statutes of limitations exist in various areas of the law. Each state/case/situation is different and must be checked carefully in current statutes.

Tolling: The start of the time period; the event that triggers the beginning of counting days/weeks/months/years for the specific statute of limitations.

Note: If the π is a minor, the time does not begin to toll until he reaches the age of majority in the state in which he lives. Of course, if a *guardian ad litem* brings a lawsuit on his behalf, that may be done before he reaches the age of majority. (See **Who Is a Person?**, page 16.)

Examples of specific statutes of limitations include:

Torts: Statutes of limitations generally range from one to six years. The interesting and unsettled issue is whether the starting time (beginning of tolling) is the time of injury or the time π first becomes aware of the injury (which could be far later). For example, in a products liability case, does the time begin to toll from the time the product was sold, the π used it first, or when a latent disease or condition (caused, π believes, by the product) was first discovered?

You can be sure that lawyers, judges, π's, and Δ's (often large companies) have debated these issues long and hard.

Very little time is given for tort claims due to government negligence (where the government is the Δ). For example, you get hit by a mail truck. These have a very short statute of limitations period. It's a matter of weeks or months!

Why is this so? Because, historically, the government had *immunity* from being sued. It did not permit itself to be sued. (See the Eleventh Amendment.) This immunity is being eroded by new laws and court decisions, but the government still sets a very short period of time in which it can be sued.

Contracts: Varies from state to state. Time generally starts tolling when the K is executed.

Criminal cases: Varies from state to state, crime to crime. There is no statute of limitations for homicides (murders, manslaughter, et cetera). That's why you read of cases prosecuted many, many years after the homicide!

The following areas are governed by federal (not state) law, according to the Constitution (See Article I, Section 8). Thus these periods are definite and uniform throughout the U.S.

Patents: Six years to sue for unauthorized use (infringement) of your patent.

Copyright: Three years to sue for copyright infringement.

Federal income tax: Three years for the IRS (Internal Revenue Service) to come after you for more taxes after the filing date or after you filed if you filed late. Thus, if you don't file your tax return, the time does not begin to toll, and the IRS can come after you without any statute of limitations! There are longer statutes of limitations for specific tax matters, omissions, et cetera. You have to check the IRC (Internal Revenue Code). Remember though, if there is fraud, no statute of limitations applies. The government's time to find you is limitless. . . . (See **Individual Income Taxes,** page 60.)

Finally, here is a concept from equity:

Laches: While no specific laws are involved, this concept prevents stale claims. Thus, even if there is no specific statute of limitations, one could use the laches defense to prevent the suit from going forward. This concept is used especially in property cases, where it's called the "Doctrine of Stale Demands." So, in law as in the kitchen, don't let things get stale!

RETROACTIVITY

Retroactivity, unlike a statute of limitations, goes backward in time. Yes, a legal time machine!

In civil cases this concept is, properly, called "retrospectivity." In criminal cases it's *ex post facto* laws. These are banned in our Constitution.

In both cases it concerns a law that relates to events or decisions in the past. In doing that it gives the earlier event a different legal effect than it had at the time it occurred.

For example, let's say a new state law requires couples applying for marriage licenses to take a blood test for AIDS. Such a law probably may not be applied retrospectively (retroactively) to married couples, as they had no expectation of such a requirement when they applied for licenses and have a vested interest in not taking it now and jeopardizing their valid license.

Generally, retroactive/retrospective laws are unconstitutional if they interfere with rights which were vested under earlier laws. That would be a "taking" without due process. (See **Legal Twosomes and Threesomes,** page 173.)

Ex post facto laws are unconstitutional. (See the Constitution, Article I, Section 9.) *Ex post facto* means "after the fact." Such a law would make an act criminal (or more severe) that was innocent (or less severe) when it occurred earlier.

Why are these laws unconstitutional (not allowed)? Simply stated, because they would be unfair. People can be prosecuted only for laws that are knowable to them. The government cannot change the rules in midstream and hold people who relied on earlier laws responsible for later ones. A Δ must be tried under the laws which existed when the crime was committed.

However, if a later law gives new or different rights, it may be given full retroactive effect.

Nunc pro tunc is another concept that goes backward in time. It means "now for then." It's a way to correct the record or a document in the past to make it be as it was supposed to be . . . and not as it actually was. Confusing? For example, if your marriage license was defective for some reason, you can by a *nunc pro tunc* order alter the license to reflect the way it was supposed to be. No, a defect in the license is not a quick and easy way to get a divorce or annulment!

FULL FAITH AND CREDIT

Good Old Article IV, Section 1 of the Constitution

Have you ever wondered why it is that if you get married in one state, you're considered married in the other forty-nine states as well? This is so even if yours is a common-law marriage, not recognized in the other states. It's so even if you don't qualify for a marriage license in another state because of its different requirements. Divorce too. Your divorce in a state with requirements totally different from another's is still valid there and everywhere else.

A driver's license, if valid in your home state, is valid in all others, even where you might not qualify for one. But this works both ways. If you lose your license in one state, you can't go to another to get one.

If you win a lawsuit in one state but the defendant's money is somewhere else, you can take your judgment to the state where the money is for collection through what's called a foreign judgment.

Why . . . why . . . why?

Why does all this work? Because of the full faith and credit clause of the Constitution. Article IV, Section 1. Different states must recognize each other's public and legal acts, records, and court decisions, and give them the same effect as where they are made initially.

This is one of those basic legal concepts that most of us don't think about too often; but when we need it, it's there!

When What Is in Your Heart and Mind Does Matter

States of Mind That Have Legal Meanings and Importance

Many cases depend on a person's mental state of being. Did the person intend to do what he did? How important is this? Extremely important. Think about it! They say even a dog knows if he has been kicked. Little children know to say, "But it was only an accident." "I didn't mean to take your bike/book/cookie."

Thus, from dogs to children, we all know that a person's state of mind is vital in assessing an event. Let's see how it plays out in specific situations in both criminal and civil law.

In criminal law, the term *mens rea* deals with the importance of a state of mind. It means a guilty mind, guilty intent. It encompasses many of the terms described below, including *intent, knowledge, malice, gross (criminal) negligence, recklessness,* among others.

Generally, a *crime* is the combination of a *mens rea* and the *actus reus* (the criminal act).

This chart gives some examples of the concepts and cases.

THE TERM	THE MEANING	RELEVANT TO	IRRELEVANT TO	DIFFERENT TYPES
CONSENT	To agree, to assent.	Medical cases. Before a procedure or medication is begun, a patient is asked to sign an "Informed Consent" for that care. If he does not, the doctor often will not provide it, for he could be later accused of a tort: assault and battery which is offensive (touching without CONSENT). In an accusation of rape, proof of the woman's consent is often the accused's best defense. The torts of assault and battery. A touch that is *unconsented* to and offensive is a *battery*. Consent searches in criminal matters. A person may consent to the search of his home, car, et cetera, but the consent must be voluntary.	In an accusation of statutory rape, the minor girl's CONSENT is no DEFENSE. A person has to be legally able to consent. See pages on children and incompetent adults. This is why parents fill out permission forms of all types for their MINOR children. The children have no legal competence to consent. A related concept is the Latin one: *volenti non fit injuria*. If a person voluntarily and knowingly exposes himself to danger or the possibility of injury or being touched, he may be deemed to have consented to that possibility. This concept comes into play with such activities as contact sports, Russian roulette, owning a dangerous animal, et cetera.	Implied Consent: This occurs when, by action, a person can be said to have agreed to something. For example, when you drive on public roads, the law implies your consent to obey the rules of the road. Your license is used as evidence of this consent. Thus, if you disobey or refuse to cooperate, your license may be taken away. This may happen with Breathalyzer tests. You have the right not to take one; but the police may remove your license! Scope of Consent: Your consent is limited to what you agreed upon. For example, in surgery, if you agreed to have your appendix removed, that's all the doctor can do. If he takes out more, that may be a tort! Express Consent: "I agree."

THE TERM	THE MEANING	RELEVANT TO	IRRELEVANT TO	DIFFERENT TYPES
				Coerced Consent: Consent that is forced under duress. Not valid. Voluntary Consent: Consent must be freely given—to be effective.
WAIVER	To give up a right, a benefit, or a privilege intentionally or voluntarily.	The right to trial by jury. This right is given to you by the Constitution in certain cases. You may *waive* the right. You have the right to be represented by a lawyer in most cases. If you want to do the case yourself, *pro se*, you may waive this right.		Express Waiver: "I waive my right . . ." Your waiver must be voluntary and with knowledge. Implied Waiver: Sometimes your actions, in not exercising a right, may imply your waiver of that right.
INTENT	To do something on purpose, willfully.	Most crimes. Your intent to do something may make it criminal, as opposed to accidental. Intent is a necessary element in most larceny crimes. *Contract* interpretation. If a term of a **K** becomes the subject of dispute between the parties, a court will attempt to figure out	Strict liability crimes or torts. In these cases, the mere fact that you did something, no matter why, may prove the crime or the tort.	

	what the parties intended at the time they entered into the **K**. See also **Wills**, page 54. When there is a dispute about the testator's will, the courts attempt to ascertain his intent. *Intentional torts,* such as assault and battery.		
MOTIVE The feeling that prompts a person to act. "I hated him." "I wanted that car."	Most crimes.		
KNOWLEDGE Generally, awareness of facts or a truth. Knowledge can be actual or inferred; actual or constructive.	Many crimes. Receipt of stolen goods. Fraud, deceit: Guilty knowledge; the intent to deceive. Also called "scienter."	Actual knowledge of all laws is not required. We are all deemed to know the laws. This is constructive knowledge. You know what they say—"Ignorance of the law is no excuse." Well, that's right!	
MALICE Generally, intentionally doing something wrong without just cause. Intentionally injuring someone. Sometimes intent is inferred from the action.	Homicide: It is the quality of mind that may mean that a homicide is a murder without malice, it may be judged a homicide.		

DEFENSES

YES—the defendant (Δ) did it.

BUT—he has an answer . . . a denial. . . .

Here, in very simplified form, are examples of defenses and samples of the types of cases where they may be relevant.

Self-Defense

"First, he came at me with a knife. Then, I was scared, so I stabbed him."

(Used in criminal/intentional tort cases.)

Defense of Property

"I warned him not to enter my home. He continued to come in. I hurt him."

(Used in criminal/intentional tort cases.)

Mistake of Fact

"I thought I was taking my own coat. I did not intend to steal yours."

(Used in criminal/tort cases.)

Insanity

"I couldn't *intend* to commit that crime, as I didn't have the *mental capacity* to know what I was doing. I couldn't control doing it or not doing it."

(Used in criminal cases.)

Infancy

"I was seven years old and didn't know any better.

The law says I didn't have the *legal capacity* to commit a crime or enter into a **K**," et cetera.

(Used in criminal/tort/**K** cases.)

Intoxication

Involuntary intoxication—

"I took a drug. I didn't know what it was or how it would affect me."

Voluntary intoxication—

"I was so drunk at that party, I didn't know what I was doing." This defense is *not* usually allowed.

(Used in criminal cases.)

Entrapment

"The undercover agent wanted to get me into trouble, so he lured me into this trap. I never would have done it on my own."

(Used in criminal cases.)

Duress

"He threatened to stab me if I didn't go with him. He forced me to do it."

(Used in criminal/wills/**K** cases.)

Truth

"Yes, I wrote and published that. Yes, I know it ruined his reputation. But it was all true."

(Used in defamation cases.)

Contributory negligence

In states that have this defense, if the plaintiff's (π's) own negligence contributed to his injury, he may not win any damages, even if the Δ was also negligent.

Comparative negligence

In states that have this defense, if π and Δ were both negligent in causing the π injuries, the π compensation (damages) is reduced by the proportion that was his fault. The Δ pays only for the portion of the injury that he caused.

Consent

"She willingly agreed to the sexual act."

"The patient agreed to have surgery performed. His *consent* was voluntary and *informed*."

"We were playing football. This means he gave his *implied consent* to being touched."

(Used in rape/tort/assault and battery cases.)

Privilege, Immunity

"You can't sue me for that statement because I said it in a court trial. It is *privileged*."

"You can't prosecute me because I am a diplomat. I have diplomatic immunity."

(Used in tort/defamation/minor criminal cases.)

CRIMINAL
LAW

FELONIES, MISDEMEANORS, AND VIOLATIONS

Criminal law is the stuff of TV shows, of good guys and bad guys. There are many different kinds of crimes, which can be classified in different ways. Here's a brief chart that helps to categorize them by their seriousness and by the severity of their punishment.

Examples of violations: Littering, jaywalking, creating a public nuisance, some zoning violations.

Examples of traffic infractions: Parking violations, and some minor moving violations, such as speeding or passing on the right.

Examples of misdemeanors: Simple assault, driving under the influence of alcohol, petty larceny, trespassing, writing a bad check.

Examples of felonies: Robbery, burglary, assault with a deadly weapon, rape, murder, perjury, killing or injuring someone while driving under the influence of alcohol or drugs.

Petty offenses do not generally appear on a person's criminal record, and are generally punishable by a fine, not imprisonment. Misdemeanors, on the other hand, go on a person's criminal record and are generally punishable by a fine and/or confinement in jail or reformatory. Felonies also go on a person's criminal record. A felon, a person convicted of a felony, loses many civil rights, including the right to vote, and may be punished by a fine and/or more than a year in prison or penitentiary, or by

117

CRIMINAL HOMICIDE

TYPE OF HOMICIDE	HOMICIDE WITH MALICE (Malice is hatred, ill will, with the *intent* to kill or to do great bodily harm.)	HOMICIDE WITH PREMEDITATION (Premeditation is a plan to do the act, no matter how quickly thought out.)	OR HOMICIDE IN CERTAIN SITUATIONS	HOMICIDE WITH ADEQUATE PROVOCATION
MURDER IN THE FIRST DEGREE	YES	YES	During a dangerous felony, such as rape, burglary, robbery, and arson. If a death occurs during these felonies, it may be a first degree murder, also known as *felony murder.*	NO
MURDER IN THE SECOND DEGREE	YES	NO. Sometimes, the accused acts in the face of known danger, such as when throwing a bomb into a crowd. While he may not plan to kill anyone in particular, if someone dies, the homicide may be a second degree murder.	During a felony such as an assault and battery.	NO
VOLUNTARY MANSLAUGHTER	NO, while there is *no malice,* there is the *intent* to kill, usually just before the killing.	NO		YES. (For example, the accused kills his spouse found in the act of adultery. The provocation is acute, as he acts in the "heat of passion," *before cooling off.)* The provocation may reduce the homicide from a possible murder to manslaughter.
INVOLUNTARY MANSLAUGHTER	NO	NO	During a *misdemeanor* or a legal act done with *criminal negligence.* (For example, the accused fights with the victim, who then falls and dies. Fighting is a legal act.)	NO
AUTOMOBILE (VEHICULAR) HOMICIDE	NO	NO	During the grossly *negligent operation* of a car. (For example, the accused may be drunk, speeds, and kills a pedestrian.)	NO

death (capital punishment), in states having the death penalty.

Treason, the most severe crime, goes on a person's criminal record, and is punishable by death, or by prison for not less than five years.

As for the places to which criminals are confined, here's a general rule: Jails and reformatories are usually reserved for less severe crimes and often are run by the city or county. Prisons and penitentiaries are usually used for more severe crimes and are run by states or by the federal government.

LARCENY: IN HOW MANY WAYS CAN SOMEONE STEAL?

Larceny is a crime made up of several elements: the taking of property (something) which belongs to someone else, without his consent and with the intent of permanently depriving him of it. Also known as *theft, stealing,* and *purloining.* The taking—from one place to another—is called "asportation."

Grand Larceny: If the property is valuable (usually over two hundred dollars).

Petit Larceny: If the property is of low value—as found in the state statute.

There are many types of larceny, as Larcenous Larry and Vicky Victim will now demonstrate:

Robbery: If Larry takes something from Vicky directly (off her body) or within her sight, with force, and against her will.

Purse snatching is a form of robbery.

Pickpocketing is *not* a form of robbery because, although Larry takes something out of Vicky's pocket, she is unaware of it and not frightened.

Armed robbery: If Larry has a lethal weapon when he robs Vicky and if Vicky believes he has one.

Extortion: If Larry uses threats or other coercion to get Vicky's money—but does not threaten her personal safety, as in *robbery*.

If, for example, he tells her he will reveal facts about her past (even if true) and she pays him to be quiet, this is *extortion*. It's also known as *blackmail*.

Burglary: If Larry takes Vicky's *property* from her house.

Breaking and Entering is the *crime* Larry commits if he enters Vicky's house with the *intent* to commit a crime there.

Embezzlement: If Larry has property entrusted to him but then takes it for himself through fraud. Here, even if he intends to give it back, it's still embezzlement.

For example, this crime may happen among employees who have money entrusted to them but falsify records, deposits, et cetera, to take the money.

Pilferage: If Larry takes small amounts (often, again and again) so his larceny won't be discovered. This crime is a problem many stores have among their employees who *pilfer* goods.

Shoplifting: If Larry takes displayed goods from a store while "shopping" there.

Thus an employee *pilfers,* while a customer *shoplifts*.

False pretenses: Getting money or property by lying with the intent to defraud. Also called "misrepresentation.'' For example: submitting phony bills; the ''white collar'' crime of fraud; submitting ''padded'' bills for reimbursement. A salesman's misrepresentation of the facts about a product, which induces a customer to buy it; e.g., if Larry, salesman, lies to Vicky about what's in the product and she buys it—based on his statements.

Misrepresentation is making a statement that is designed to deceive or mislead someone.

Bad checks are a form of *false pretenses* called ''uttering.'' Larry writes a *bad check* if he knows there is no money in his account to cover it.

Receipt of stolen property: If Larry's friend gets the goods and *knows* they are stolen. The crime can also occur if a stranger buys the goods from Larry, while knowing they are stolen.

Mistake of fact is not larceny: If Larry takes Vicky's property but thinks it is his own, there is no larceny because he had no *intent* to deprive Vicky of her property. This may happen at a restaurant, if Larry takes the wrong umbrella.

Note: The key to *larceny* crimes is the *intent* to deprive the owner of his property. However, this is not true for embezzlement, as shown above. Note also that the key to *receipt of stolen property* is *knowledge* that the property is ''hot.''

HOMICIDE

Homicide is the killing of one person by someone else. Here are some examples.

—A shoots B and kills him.

—C kills D while driving under the influence of alcohol (DWI).

—E kills F in self-defense.

—G fights with H. H falls, hits his head, and dies.

These are all homicides. But, are they all criminal homicides? If so, are they examples of murder or manslaughter?

Punishment for the different homicides varies greatly. Note that of all homicides, first-degree murder is the most serious—and punished most severely.

Follow the chart below to analyze how the laws of homicide work—and make some sense of the news you hear and your favorite TV show!

There are three broad categories of homicides:

1. **Justifiable**
   —by a soldier in wartime.
   —by court order (such as execution).
   —when necessary to prevent a felony, stop a riot, catch a felon.

2. Excusable
—as a result of an accident or a mistake.
—as a result of ordinary *negligence*. (As in a car accident. But see below for *gross negligence*.)
—by someone who has no *legal capacity* to commit the crime (such as a child).

3. Criminal
—is neither justifiable nor excusable.

State laws divide criminal homicide into different categories. While these differ from state to state, a generalized pattern is summarized below.

PUNISHMENT

CRIME—INDICTMENT—TRIAL/GUILTY PLEA/PLEA BARGAIN—CONVICTION—PUNISHMENT

Punishment is the penalty for a *crime*. The *court's punishment order* is called the *sentence*.

"I sentence you to . . ."

Note that the terminology for the person punished changes during the criminal sequence. Before the indictment he is the "accused." After the indictment, before the conviction, he is the "defendant" (Δ). Following conviction (or guilty plea), he is the "convict."

Criminal law sometimes is called penal law (punishment law).

Jails and prisons are sometimes called "penal institutions." An example from history: Australia was used by the British government as a penal colony for prisoners. Apparently it was preferable to send prisoners "down under" than to incarcerate them back home!

Punishments include:

Capital Punishment: The death penalty. (Your head is your "capital.")

Corporal Punishment: Physical punishment, such as lashing. (Your "corpus" is your body.)

Imprisonment/Incarceration: Confinement in a jail or prison (or anywhere against your will, actually).

Determinate Sentence/Indeterminate Sentence: A determinate sentence is for a fixed time period, as determined by statute. The statute lists the number of months or years of incarceration for specific crimes.

Indeterminate sentences have fixed minimum and maximum time periods within that range. The actual length of time a person may serve is set by the statutes, officials, and the prisoner's behavior. You've heard of "time off for good behavior." This may occur with an indeterminate sentence.

Parole: Release from jail or prison after serving part of a sentence. The release is conditional on the convict's behavior outside prison. If he violates the terms of his release, it may be revoked. In that case he "violates parole" and may be reincarcerated.

Fine: A sum of money a convict pays to the court. (This money is different from damages, which a Δ pays a plaintiff, π.)

Restitution: An order that the convict restore the victim's property. Example: by paying for repair of damage or by the return of specific items.

Suspended sentence: A prison term that a convict does not actually serve in prison. Instead, he is placed on probation. If he violates the terms of probation, then he is sent to serve the term.

Probation: Letting the convict serve his term outside prison, during good behavior and, usually, under the supervision of a probation officer. If the convict violates the terms of his probation, he may be incarcerated. Note that generally parole occurs after a convict has been incarcerated for some time, while probation occurs instead of incarceration. The word *probation* comes from the Latin: proving something. It appears also in "probating" a will (proving its authenticity); or a "probationary" period at work to see if the new employee will work out well. In the case of criminal law it gives a convict a chance to prove his good behavior. The word *parole* has a Latin root that means to speak. Here the convict promises (says) he will behave himself. Interesting difference.

Following a court's sentencing order the executive branch (the governor of a state or the President of the U.S.) sometimes (rarely) steps in to change that order, through the power of executive clemency. There are three types:

1. Pardon: The best! Declares the person innocent. Wipes the slate clean. Clears the person's criminal record.

2. Commutation of sentence: Reduces the punishment. Example: by shortening the prison term or changing a sentence of capital punishment to imprisonment.

3. Reprieve: A temporary suspension in the punishment. Example: to give the convict time to settle his business, deal with family matters, and so on, before he starts a prison term. It's also a stay of execution of a pending death penalty, often to give a prisoner more time for further appeals to court.

Finally, remember, the Constitution limits punishments in key ways:

The Eighth Amendment guarantees that there shall be no "cruel and unusual punishment." The definition of "cruel and unusual" changes over time and is left for the courts to define. Now it generally means punishment that is so disproportionate to the crime that it offends our notions of fundamental fairness. That's pretty clear, isn't it! But it means you probably won't go to jail for jaywalking, and torture is considered "cruel."

The Fifth Amendment protects Δ's against *double jeopardy*. This means that if a Δ is found innocent by a court, he may not be tried again for the same offense. However, if the first trial ended in a *hung jury* (no verdict), he may be tried again. He was not acquitted. If the first case was in state court, he may be tried for the same offense in federal court. Remember, too, that even if a Δ is acquitted in a criminal case, he may still be sued civilly by a victim(s) or other π's. That would not be a case of double jeopardy.

The language of the Amendment is picturesque:

. . . nor shall any person be subject for the same offence to be twice put in jeopardy of life or limb.

LEGAL PROCEDURES AND COURTS

WHO'S WHO IN THE COURTROOM

A courtroom can be an overwhelming place, with its formality and its procedures and its people. Lots of people do different jobs there. Some of them are employed by the court; others play a role in the specific proceeding. Here's a who's who that may help.

Prosecution: The government (state, local, or federal) that brings a defendant (Δ) to trial for a crime.

Plaintiff (π): The person who sues a Δ.

Defendant (Δ): In a criminal case the person charged with a crime. In a civil case the person sued by the π.

Parties: The π and Δ. Each is a party in a civil case. Also called litigants. There may be more than one π or Δ. There may be a large group of π's or Δ's who don't even know each other, as in a class action suit. (See page 144.)

Witness: A person called by either party in a civil case or by either side in a criminal case to give evidence, through testimony, to the court. The witness testifies (answers questions) under oath.

There are many types of witnesses, including:

1. Character witness: A witness who vouches for the character and standing in the community of a party or Δ, but who does not know about the specific case before the court.

2. Expert witness: A witness with special knowledge, experience, or training in the field about which he testifies. An expert witness is permitted to give his opinion in court, unlike a lay witness who generally does not give an opinion.

3. Lay witness: A witness generally called to testify about what he saw firsthand or to impart other firsthand knowledge he may have.

4. Material witness: In a criminal case the witness whose testimony is vital to prove the guilt or innocence of the Δ.

5. Hostile witness: A witness who is biased against the party or side questioning him.

Judge: A public officer with authority to hear and decide cases in court.

Bailiff: A court attendant who maintains order in court. He's the one who shouts, ''Order in the court!''

Clerk: A court officer who files documents with the court (such as motions and pleadings), keeps records of all legal proceedings, and generally knows what's going on. If you have questions about the court's procedures, ask the clerk!

Law clerk: A person, often a young lawyer, who helps the judge with research and writing decisions and other documents.

Jury: A group of laypersons who decide the facts in a case at trial. A jury may have six or twelve members, depending on the court and state involved. Called a petit jury, as opposed to the grand jury in criminal cases, which brings an indictment or a no bill. (See **Basic Pro-**

cedure in a Criminal Case, page 136 and **Jurisdiction,** page 95.)

Lawyer: Also called attorney, counsel, advocate, and possibly other names, as well. . . . The person hired to represent his client's interests to achieve a specific legal goal. Remember, the client is the employer—not the other way around!

A lawyer is also considered an "officer of the court," with an obligation to do justice. As you can imagine, these roles may sometimes be challenging and can create conflicts for lawyers.

Prosecuting attorney: Also called district attorney, assistant district attorney, and government's lawyer. The lawyer prosecuting a criminal case for the government (The People) or representing the government in any other matter.

Bar: The railing separating the participants in a trial from the observers. Lawyers are called members of the bar. To disbar a lawyer is to revoke his license to practice law.

Magistrate: A judge (sometimes called a judicial officer) of a lower court, dealing with misdemeanor cases—for example, a justice of the peace.

Sheriff: A law officer of a county who serves summonses, subpoenas, and other legal documents and carries out judgments of the court. A sheriff also calls jurors. (See **When the Sheriff Is at the Door**, page 151.)

Deputy sheriff: A person appointed by the sheriff to assist him.

The following officials may function in administrative agencies, not courts (see **Jurisdiction**, page 95).

Hearing officer: Also called hearing examiner or administrative law judge. A public officer with authority to hear and decide cases in an administrative agency. Examples of these agencies include the tax agencies, labor boards, real estate boards, social security, special education, et cetera.

DOCUMENTS

Lawyers can, and often do, bury you in paper.
Eek—Here's a *summons!*
Oh—Here's a contract, a subpoena!
Now what?
What are all these papers?

Since law is a profession of words, it is vital to understand the type of document with which you are dealing. A document is a paper with *legal* significance.

Are you signing away your fortune or proving that you have one? Are you asking the court to move the trial or is the court forcing you to move?

Here are some common and basic types of documents, each with its own purpose, limits, and significance. . . .

Affidavit: A written statement of facts sworn to under oath and signed in front of a person authorized to administer an oath, such as a notary public.

The person writing it is called the *affiant*. The part

signed by the notary is called the *jurat,* and says something like:

Sworn before me this ——— day of ——— 19———
at ———.

Bill: This little word has many legal meanings. Among these are:

It may be a *law* in draft form; that is, before it is passed by the *legislature,* while it is debated before enactment (when a bill becomes a law).

It is the Bill of Rights that sets out many basic rights and freedoms.

It may be something we all know very well—a statement of money owed. Too often, the mailbox is full of bills!

Certificate: A document stating a fact, qualification, promise, et cetera. For example: A *teaching certificate* permits a person to teach in the state (jurisdiction) of the certificate; a *marriage certificate* states the person is married (in all jurisdictions). (See **Full Faith and Credit,** page 107, and **Jurisdiction,** page 95.) Note: In some places these are called "licenses." See below.

Charter: An act of the legislature that sets up a corporation. Called "certificate of incorporation." A *city charter,* which creates a city, is also set up by the legislature.

Contract: An agreement between people or corporations or other entities that can be enforced by a court. It is usually written, but not always. (See **Contracts,** page 39.)

Decree: A judgment of a court. An order. For example: A *divorce decree* ends a marriage.

Deed: A writing that transfers ownership of land and buildings from one person to another (the grantor to the grantee). (See **Real Estate: The Law of Home Sweet Home,** page 73.)

Indictment: A written accusation by a grand jury, stating that there is enough evidence against a person to charge him with a crime.

Interrogatories: A pretrial discovery tool used in civil cases. It is a set of written questions that one party serves—don't you love that word!—on the other. The questions are answered under oath.

License: A document giving official permission to do something. For example: A *driver's license* permits a person to drive; a license to practice medicine in the jurisdiction covered by the license lets a person be a doctor there. (Note: As with certificates, some licenses are limited to specific jurisdictions.) (See **Jurisdiction,** page 95.)

Motion: An application to a court for a ruling or an order. For example: A motion to change the trial location is a change of venue motion. A motion to strike asks the judge to remove specific testimony from the record. (See **Verbs in Court,** page 159.)

Order: A command or decision by a judge. (See **Verbs in Court,** page 161.)

Ordinance: A municipal (city) law. (See **Laws, Statutes, Regulations, and Canons,** page 11.)

Record: The history of a court action. All the testimony, documents, and other evidence presented.

Statute: A law passed by state or federal legislatures. (See page 11.)

Subpoena: A written order or writ requiring the person to whom it is addressed to appear in court to give testimony (called a *subpoena ad testificandum*) and/or to bring specific documents or other evidence (called a *subpoena duces tecum*). (See page 152.)

Summons: Written notice to a person or persons or corporation or other entity that there is a lawsuit against him/her/them/it. The document that starts an action when served upon the Δ. (See page 151.)

Testament: Any proof that serves as evidence of something. For example, a last will and testament proves how the decedent (person who died) wanted his property (called "estate") distributed after his death. (See **Wills,** page 54.)

Warrant: A writ or order authorizing an officer to make an arrest, conduct a search of a person or premises or seize property belonging to a Δ, or perform another task. Examples are bench warrants, search warrants, arrest warrants.

Will: A document that states how a person wants to dispose of (divide, give away) his property ("estate") after death. (See page 54.)

Writ: A formal document ordering an action. Usually, it orders an officer of the state to do something. For example, writ of habeas corpus, writ of certiorari, writ of execution.

Writ of habeas corpus: The Great Writ. An order that a person appear in court to determine if he is held in custody legally.

Writ of execution: A court order to enforce a judgment granted to the π by authorizing the sheriff to impose a levy on property, in the court's jurisdiction, that belongs to the judgment debtor (Δ).

Writ of certiorari: An order by a higher court to a lower court to get the record of proceedings so that the higher court can review the lower court's decision for error.

BASIC PROCEDURE IN A
CRIMINAL CASE

TOM HAS A LARGE AMOUNT OF ILLEGAL DRUGS. THE POLICE SEARCH HIS APARTMENT AS A RESULT OF INFORMATION FROM A RELIABLE SOURCE.

Below is a summary of the steps that may be used in the *felony* prosecution of his case. (Misdemeanors are treated differently.) (See page 117.) Note: The states

BASIC PROCEDURE IN A CRIMINAL CASE

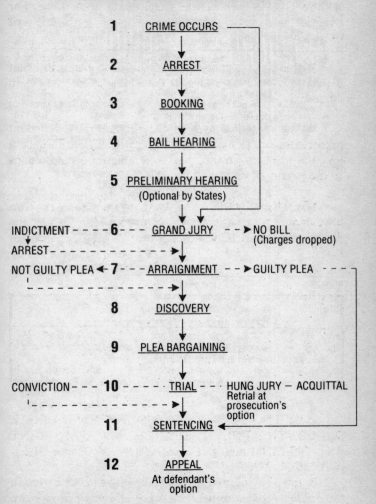

1 <u>CRIME OCCURS</u>

2 <u>ARREST</u>

3 <u>BOOKING</u>

4 <u>BAIL HEARING</u>

5 <u>PRELIMINARY HEARING</u>
(Optional by States)

INDICTMENT - - - - **6** - - - <u>GRAND JURY</u> - - ▶ NO BILL
(Charges dropped)

ARREST - - - - - - - - - - - - ▶

NOT GUILTY PLEA ◀ - - - **7** - - - <u>ARRAIGNMENT</u> - - ▶ GUILTY PLEA - - -

8 <u>DISCOVERY</u>

9 <u>PLEA BARGAINING</u>

CONVICTION - - - **10** - - - - <u>TRIAL</u> - - HUNG JURY — ACQUITTAL
Retrial at
prosecution's
option

11 <u>SENTENCING</u> ◀

12 <u>APPEAL</u>
At defendant's
option

differ in the details described. Some steps may be eliminated, changed, added, et cetera.

STEP	WHAT HAPPENS	TOM'S RIGHTS AND THEIR CONSTITUTIONAL SOURCES
ARREST	Tom is taken into custody by the police or other citizen. This means he loses his personal freedom (the right to come and go as he pleases). He is under the jurisdiction of the court. (See page 95.)	Before questioning him police must inform Tom of his rights, the "Miranda rights," which include: —the right to have a lawyer present —the right to remain silent (not answer any questions) —the right to know that anything he says or does may be used against him in court. These rights are based on the Fifth Amendment's guarantee. A Δ cannot be forced to be a witness against himself. Sixth Amendment: Δ's right to an attorney's presence in criminal cases.
BOOKING . . . at police station	Tom's name and the nature of the alleged crime are recorded in the police ledger (book).	
BAIL HEARING . . . before a judge or magistrate	Tom applies for bail. Bail is money or property paid or pledged to the court to assure that he will appear for trial. If bail is granted, Tom is free to leave until his next hearing date. Tom may be released without bail—ROR—Released on his Own Recognizance—if the judge believes his promise to appear at trial, or for other reasons. If bail is denied or if Tom can't pay the amount, he may wait in jail until his next court	Eighth Amendment. Excessive bail cannot be required. Article I, Section 9, of the Constitution. Tom has the right to apply for a writ of *habeas corpus* if he believes he is being held unjustly.

STEP	WHAT HAPPENS	TOM'S RIGHTS AND THEIR CONSTITUTIONAL SOURCES
	date. Bail may be denied if the court believes Tom is unlikely to appear for trial or for other reasons.	
PRELIMINARY HEARING . . . before a judge or magistrate	Used in some jurisdictions. The judge or magistrate decides whether to send the case to the grand jury, to charge Tom with the crime, or to release him.	
GRAND JURY	This is a group of twenty-three citizens who meet to investigate and decide whether to accuse Tom of a crime. The grand jury hears only the evidence the prosecution presents. Tom does not have to appear. If there is enough evidence, the grand jury may issue an indictment, which is a formal written accusation. (Also called a *true bill*.) If not, a *no bill* is issued, the charges are dropped, and Tom is released. Following an indictment, if the Δ is not in custody, he may be arrested at this time.	Fifth Amendment: A grand jury indictment is guaranteed in all serious felonies. The purpose of indictments is to prevent the government from bringing a Δ to trial without enough evidence.
ARRAIGNMENT . . . before a judge	Tom appears before a judge, who advises him of the grand jury charge(s). Tom may plead guilty or not guilty. If he pleads not guilty, he can again apply for bail. (See page 138.)	Sixth Amendment: In all criminal cases, the accused has the right to know the accusation against him. Eighth Amendment applies again. (See page 138.) Article I, Section 9, *habeas corpus* applies. (See page 136.)
DISCOVERY	Tom and his lawyer may seek information from the prosecution about the case against him. He may ask for:	Fourth Amendment: Searches and seizures are to be conducted with a search warrant upon a showing of

STEP	WHAT HAPPENS	TOM'S RIGHTS AND THEIR CONSTITUTIONAL SOURCES
	—Bill of Particulars (stating the time, place, and manner/means of the alleged crime). —list of witnesses. —grand jury minutes. —statements made by witnesses. —statements made by Δ that the prosecution has. —tangible evidence. In this case, the drugs. 　　Tom may file motions, such as —Motion for further particulars —Motion to suppress evidence illegally obtained —Motion to dismiss the case 　　In some jurisdictions there is some reciprocity for discovery by the prosecution.	probable cause. (There are some exceptions.) 　　If a search/seizure is illegal, the evidence obtained from it cannot be used. This is the "fruit-of-the-poisonous tree" doctrine. (See page 179.)
PLEA BARGAINING	Tom and the prosecution may (in some cases) negotiate a settlement of the case. Tom may plead guilty to the crime charged or to a lesser crime. His attorney and the prosecution may agree on a disposition (settlement) of the case. This may involve jail, a fine, restitution, and/or community service. The court may, but is not required to, accept the agreed-upon disposition.	
TRIAL . . . by a judge or jury Tom chooses between a jury and judge trial.	This is the court proceeding to decide if Tom is guilty or not guilty of the charges against him. 　　The prosecution may present testimony, docu-	Sixth Amendment. Right to a speedy and public trial. If the trial is not held soon, Tom may file for a writ of *habeas corpus*. 　　Sixth Amendment. Tom

STEP	WHAT HAPPENS	TOM'S RIGHTS AND THEIR CONSTITUTIONAL SOURCES
This is called the *petit jury*. (See page 130.)	ments, and tangible evidence. Tom may question (cross-examine) witnesses against him. He may call witnesses in his favor. He decides whether to testify.	has the right to an *impartial* jury. Sixth Amendment. Tom has the right to call witnesses for and against him. He can *subpoena* (order them to appear). Fifth Amendment. Tom has the right to remain silent. His refusal to testify ("taking the Fifth") cannot be used as evidence against him. Tom has the right to be *presumed innocent until proven guilty*.
VERDICT	The decision by the judge or jury. This may be a finding of guilty or not guilty. If a jury cannot reach a verdict, this is called a "hung jury." If Tom is acquitted (found not guilty), he is released.	Fifth Amendment guarantees that Tom cannot be retried for the same crime if he is found not guilty: This is the right against "double jeopardy." Note: After a "hung jury," he may be retried.
SENTENCING	If Tom is found guilty, he will be sentenced by the judge according to the state's *penal code*.	Eighth Amendment guarantees that punishment cannot be "cruel and unusual." (See page 126.)
APPEAL	Tom may appeal a guilty verdict. The prosecution may not appeal a not-guilty verdict.	Fifth Amendment guarantee against double jeopardy. See above.

BASIC PROCEDURE IN A CIVIL CASE

Tom, a wholesaler, and Bob, a retailer, enter into a contract for the sale of spring clothing for Bob's store. Tom breaches (fails to carry out) the K and doesn't deliver the clothing on time. Bob starts a lawsuit to get damages for the loss sustained because of Tom's breach.

Below is a summary of the steps that *may* be used in the civil lawsuit. Bob is the π; Tom, the Δ. Please note that these procedures are very general; they differ from state to state and from situation to situation.

1. An event occurs.

Note: Not all wrongs have legal remedies! Bob needs to be sure he has a cause of action recognized by law.

2. Lawsuit begins by π's notice to Δ, including a complaint and summons.

These are vital to the American legal system, as they embody the very essence of due process. In most cases Tom (Δ) has a right to notice of the suit against him, so he can prepare to challenge it. An exception may be if Bob attaches Tom's house, bank account, or other property before Tom gets notice of that action. Attachment is a legal process by court action, for taking property into the court's custody. It may be used if deemed necessary to assure payment of the judgment, should Bob ultimately win.

BASIC PROCEDURE IN A CIVIL CASE

1 An event occurs, such as a breach of K, a tort, or other civil wrong.

2 Lawsuit begins by π's notice to Δ, including a COMPLAINT and SUMMONS.

3 From this action, other suits may emerge, such as a COUNTER SUIT, a CROSS SUIT, or a THIRD PARTY SUIT.

4 TRIAL PREPARATION
PRE-TRIAL DISCOVERY

Which may include:

- Interrogatories
- Deposition
- Request for Production
- Examination of a Witness
- Request for Admissions

5 SETTLEMENT

The parties may try to settle their dispute at any time.

If a party fails to cooperate with DISCOVERY, the opposing party may seek COURT action through a MOTION TO COMPEL. Once a MOTION is GRANTED by a COURT, if the noncooperation persists, COURT may impose SANCTIONS for CONTEMPT.

6 PRETRIAL CONFERENCE
SUMMARY JUDGMENT
DEFAULT

7 TRIAL
DIRECTED VERDICT

8 VERDICT
JUDGMENT N.O.V.

9 APPEAL

3. Other suits may emerge from this lawsuit. Here are some examples:

Countersuit: Tom, the Δ in Bob's lawsuit, may sue Bob. For example, he may sue for the money Bob still owed him from the winter shipment. In this case Tom will be the π and Bob the Δ.

Cross claim: In a lawsuit with more than one π or Δ, a claim by one party against a coparty. (A π suing another π.)

Third-party complaint: A complaint filed by the Δ against a party not involved in the case (the third party) alleging that the third party may be liable for the damages that the π might win against the Δ. It can get complex!

Class action lawsuit: An action that needs court approval and must follow specific rules. It is brought by one or more members of a large group of π's or against a large group of Δ's. All members of the class must receive notice of it; all members (unless they opt to remove themselves from the class) are bound by the judgment.

These rules in the federal courts are found in *Rule 23 of Civil Procedure*. Most state courts have similar Rule 23 class action suits.

For example, a few stockholders in a corporation may sue on behalf of all stockholders whose stock value fell because of an insider-trading deal.

Other examples of class-action suits include those involving environmental pollution or cases in the consumer protection area (for example, all consumers harmed by the use of a particular product).

The purpose of countersuits, cross suits, third-party suits, and class-action suits is to avoid multiple litigation by getting everyone in court at the same time.

4. Trial preparation

Pretrial discovery. Procedures by which the parties to a lawsuit may obtain relevant information to prepare their cases. The purpose here is twofold: to produce more efficient (and quicker) trials and/or to produce settlements, as each side can assess the strength and weakness of his case.

Discovery rules are extensively defined in both the Federal Rules (for federal cases) and different state rules.

Interrogatories: Written questions about the case submitted by one party to the other or to a witness. These are answered under oath. (The person answering the questions signs a statement that the answers are true.)

Deposition: Oral questions asked by one party of the other or of a witness. The party deposed is the ''deponent.'' The deposition is conducted under oath outside the courtroom (usually in a lawyer's office). A word-for-word record is made and written, called the transcript.

Request for production: Request for documents, photographs, or other tangible materials in the possession of a party by the other party. The requesting party may seek to inspect, copy, and review this material.

Different state rules exist regarding the need for a court order for such a request.

Physical examination of a witness: Permitted only when the condition of a witness is critical to the case, as following a car accident or medical procedure. It is performed by the other party's medical or other expert.

Again, states differ on a need for a court order.

Request for admissions: An admission is a voluntary statement that something is true. Written statements of facts submitted by one party to the other, which he must admit or refute. Those statements admitted are taken as true and need not be proven at trial. In some states, if the party fails to respond or refute the statements, the statements are deemed to be admitted.

Sanctions: A penalty for failing to comply with a discovery order. The sanction may be a fine or imprisonment. Several famous cases recently have incarcerated parents for failing to inform the court of the whereabouts of their children. In these cases, often dealings with suspected child abuse the parents claimed that they feared for the child's safety if his whereabouts were made known.

Contempt order: Sanctions may be ordered when a person disobeys a court order or in other ways interferes with the dignity of the court.

5. Settlement: The parties may, at any time, attempt to compromise the case; to settle it.

6. Pretrial conference: A meeting called by the judge between the lawyers for both parties, which attempts either to settle the case or to narrow the issues for the trial. Most cases settle at some point before a trial. If they didn't, our court dockets would be even fuller than they are! In this way the judicial system relies on the fact that most cases will never proceed to trial.

Summary judgment: Either party may, before the trial begins, move for a summary judgment. If granted, this means that the case may be decided on the basis of the law involved, and that no facts need be presented. Or put another way, even if one party's facts are totally believed as true, it would make no difference; the result is already knowable by applying specific laws. The judge may then apply the laws and issue a summary judgment.

7. Trial: The court proceeding to determine whether the π or the Δ has met its burden of proof by a preponderance of evidence. (See page 102.) Note how different this is from a criminal case, where only the *prosecution* has the burden of proof against the Δ. There, the Δ does *not* need to prove he is not guilty.

The Seventh Amendment of the Constitution grants the right to a trial by jury in a civil case involving over twenty dollars in controversy. In practice, however, most small cases do not have a jury trial because of the expense involved. Different states have different rules for the availability of a right to a trial by jury.

At trial each side may present an opening statement, witnesses, documents, and other evidence. Each side may question (examine) witnesses directly, through cross-examination and rebuttal. Finally, each side may present a closing statement.

Directed verdict: Before the verdict either side may move for a directed verdict. This means the judge finds that the party who had to prove its case (who had the burden of proof) did not even make a *prima facie* case. (See page 101.) The judge may order the jury to find for the other party.

8. Verdict: The jury renders its decision, based on the civil law standard of proof. (**Civil and Criminal Laws,** page 10.) In a jury-waived or nonjury trial, the judge renders the decision.

Judgment n.o.v. (non obstante veredicto): A judgment notwithstanding the verdict. Good old Latin! Either party may move the court to grant such a judgment in a jury trial if the verdict clearly makes no sense (couldn't possibly be based on the facts presented). Then, if granted, the judge may grant a directed verdict for the moving party. As you can imagine, judgments n.o.v. are relatively rare.

Appeal: Either side may request that a higher court review the trial court's verdict.

SMALL CLAIMS COURT

Let's say Sam takes his shirts to the cleaners. Five of them are fine, but three are ruined. The cleaners will assume no responsibility for the damage. What can he do?

Sue buys a new table. When she gets home, she discovers many scratches on it. The store won't take it back.

Betsy's landlord won't return her security deposit after she moves out of the apartment.

In these cases, and countless others like them, what can folks do? They have several options, such as: they can try to settle the problem with the other side, forget about it, or sue in small claims court.

Small claims courts are designed to provide an informal, fast, and inexpensive way to settle disputes. They are used in uncomplicated civil cases that involve relatively small dollar amounts. Generally, a person can sue someone without using a lawyer. However, it may be worthwhile to consult a lawyer before proceeding with a case, to assess the case and strategies to use.

The first and very basic issue is: Do you have a case? In legalese: Do you have a cause of action? Remember, just because something bad happened does not mean it's anyone's fault legally. Just because you are (even rightfully) mad doesn't mean the court can help you. The basic question is: Has the Δ done a legal wrong for which the π can sue? Usually, this means that you have to sue on a legal theory, such as negligence, breach of K, implied warranty, and so on.

Every state sets its own maximum for which someone can sue in small claims court. These maximums ranged, in 1990, from around one thousand dollars to five thousand dollars. Most states' limits are between one thousand and three thousand dollars. To find out the maximum in any state, call the clerk of the small claims court.

In these courts the judge or arbitrator decides the entire matter: both the facts involved and the applicable law. (See page 99.) In some states parties may appeal these decisions to higher courts; in others they may not.

Here is a summary of the procedure involved:

1. The plaintiff (π) fills out a complaint or claim against the defendant (Δ). This document states the basic facts and what the π seeks to win. Many times the court has a standard form that should be used. Call the clerk to get one.

2. The π pays a filing fee to the court. If the Δ loses, he may have to reimburse the π later.

3. The π gets a hearing date and a case number from the clerk.

4. The π gets the complaint delivered to the Δ, usually by having the clerk mail it with a summons or by having the sheriff deliver it. The summons orders the Δ to answer the complaint by a certain date. It is the π's responsibility to have the complaint delivered by any means necessary, as he cannot proceed in court without that. Remember the basic due process notice requirements in American law!

5. The Δ may offer to settle the case or may, in some states, file his answer (also called "response"). In some states the Δ need not file an answer at all. At this time the Δ may choose to settle or use the answer to prepare his case.

6. Either party may ask the clerk for a continuance (postponement) if he/they cannot appear in court on the assigned date.

7. On the assigned date, both parties should appear in court at the proper time. Otherwise they risk losing by default. As in sports, if one side fails to appear in court, he may lose and get a default judgment against him.

8. Both parties should prepare their case by having the appropriate documents and witnesses. Documents may include sales slips, photos of damage, advertising that was relied on, letters, and anything else that may prove the case.

9. Depending on the judge or arbitrator and state where the case is heard, both parties may be allowed to present their story, with the π proceeding first, present witnesses, question the witnesses of the other side, answer the questions posed by the judge or arbitrator, and so on.

10. The judge or arbitrator may announce the decision at the end of the hearing or may send it within a few days. If the π wins, he will get an order, called a judgment, against the Δ for a specific amount of money or another form of payment. The Δ now becomes the judgment debtor.

11. Now starts the challenge of collecting on that judgment!

Remember: Procedures vary from state to state. Visit a small claims court in your area to see how the process works. It's the best way to prepare for your day in court.

WHEN THE SHERIFF IS AT THE DOOR

You're at home. Minding your own business. All is relaxed, until the knock at the door. It's someone with a *summons, subpoena,* or *warrant* for YOU. It could be the sheriff, marshal, or other peace officer, a process server, someone you know or a stranger. What's going on? What should you do?

Are you being sued? Did you commit a crime or offense? Are you being called as a witness in court? It could be any of these events. . . .

IN A CIVIL MATTER (See page 142.)

The person at the door is "serving" you with a legal *document,* such as a summons, subpoena, warrant, or writ.

Service of process is the delivery of such a document by hand or mail. (Lawyers are ever so polite! They speak of "serving" the summons, et cetera.)

1. Summons (called *summons and complaint* in federal courts) informs the *defendant* (Δ) that he is being sued and tells him how, when, and where to defend himself.

Note: Anyone at home may be handed the summons and "served." Yes, even a child of "appropriate age" (the age differs from state to state). Refusing to take the summons or throwing it away may have no effect. It has still been "served."

Sometimes, as in *small claims court, a summons* may be delivered by registered or certified mail (with a return receipt request). Here, in contrast to the above, if the Δ does not receive the letter (or, knowing what it is, refuses to sign for it), then the *summons* may not be deemed "served."

The important concepts to remember about *service of process* are the notice and *due process* requirements of American law. *Notice* of the legal action to the party affected is critical. (Except in attachments. See page 142.) The party sued or subpoenaed must be notified through an appropriate *service of process*. Once so served, he may be subject to the court's *jurisdiction*. Without proper service his *due process* rights cannot be exercised. Without notice the Δ or *witness* is not subject to the court's *jurisdiction*. The proceedings cannot continue.

The *document* server fills out a *Proof of Service* under oath, stating the time, place, and manner of service. This *Proof of Service* becomes part of the *record* in the case.

Once served, what should a person do? He has to respond somehow: by appearing as directed, by seeking a postponement, by filing an *answer*. At this time he should probably consult an attorney before he does anything.

What if the Δ doesn't appear in court, even after being properly served? The penalty for not showing up may be a *default judgment*. That is, he may lose simply by not *making an appearance*.

2. A **subpoena** is a *writ* (written order, see pages 136) issued by a court or other authority, that compels a person to appear in court, at a hearing or other proceeding, as a *witness*.

3. A **subpoena duces tecum** requires the *witness* to bring specific materials with him. For example, an office manager may be required to bring all sales receipts or time sheets for a given period of time.

Once served, if a witness does not appear, he may be punished for contempt of court. (See below for **bench warrant.**)

IN A CRIMINAL MATTER
(See page 136.)

The sheriff or marshal at the door could deliver any of the following:

4. Warrant: This is a writ from a competent authority such as a judge or magistrate directing someone to do something specific, such as arrest a person or search a specific place or thing.

5. Arrest Warrant: A warrant to seize a person and bring him to court or to inform him when to appear in court.

If the person fails to appear as required, the judge may issue a *bench warrant* for his arrest. This may be issued if a person fails to appear in court to answer a charge or if a *witness* fails to appear in response to a *subpoena*. (See above.)

6. A **search warrant** is based on a law officer's sworn statement, describing the place or thing (such as an apartment or car) to be searched for specific items. The Constitution guarantees that both *search* and *arrest warrants* may be issued only on the basis of *probable cause*. This means that it is *reasonable* to believe that a crime has been committed (or will be committed) as stated or that certain property is required.

Note: Many lawyers and judges have spent years of their lives, and much law exists, defining the meanings and procedures involved: *probable cause, reasonableness, unreasonable search,* et cetera. It is a very complex and fascinating area of the law.

Meanwhile, back to the doorway. If the items sought are found as specified, they may be used as *evidence* in a *criminal trial* or destroyed as *contraband*. If a search is conducted without a proper warrant, or evidence not specified is found, the evidence so collected may not be used in court. That evidence may be what is called "the fruit of the poisonous tree." Caveat: This is a complex area of law and each situation is unique. (See **Jargon,** page 179.)

Note also: Generally, in criminal cases, there may be situations when a warrant is not required. This may be if the person is likely to disappear or if the *evidence* is likely to be destroyed, or if the person may be dangerous and is likely to commit a crime.

At such times the officer may make a forced entry or arrest without *warrant,* for example. These situations are generally called "exigent circumstances" (emergency situations). Specific rules and guidelines apply in all cases, which differ from jurisdiction to jurisdiction.

ALTERNATIVE DISPUTE RESOLUTION, OR ADR

I'LL SEE YOU IN COURT! OR WILL I? INTRODUCING . . . ALTERNATIVE DISPUTE RESOLUTION!!!

There are several ways to settle legal disputes without going to court. They are called alternative dispute resolution models.

Alternative to what? (A) To litigation: the judicial (court) contest that decides and enforces legal rights. (B) To the adversary system: another name for litigation. People usually use ADR because it is less time consuming, less expensive, and less stressful than litigation.

ADR currently exists in several forms: negotiation, arbitration, conciliation, mediation, pretrial hearings.

1. Negotiation: Occurs when the parties try to settle their dispute themselves. Just as between parents and children, husbands and wives or neighbors and colleagues, it is a possible avenue for resolving disputes that involve legal rights and responsibilities.

2. Conciliation: Occurs in court before trial, when the parties meet to try to settle their differences. If they do so, they are said to "reach a settlement agreement."

Also used in labor disputes before the arbitration as a final effort to settle the case.

3. Pretrial hearing or conference: Occurs when the parties meet before the trial begins to settle their dispute or narrow the issues between them or agree on certain facts ("stipulations"), to simplify the trial.

This meeting usually occurs with the judge or administrative hearing officer who will hear the case if it doesn't settle.

4. Mediation: Occurs when the disputing parties try to settle their differences by having a neutral third person, a mediator, help them. The mediator may be a stranger or friend or someone hired by the parties through a mediation service. The mediator

—hears both sides,
—listens to each side privately (in what is called a "caucus"),
—brings the parties together,
—helps them see their areas of agreement as well as disagreement, so they may settle their dispute.

Mediation may be used often in divorce cases and in relatively minor criminal matters, as when neighbors argue about unruly children or dogs, or in assault and battery situations among family members or schoolmates. It is often used by people who know each other and need to get along in the future. A court may order the parties to attempt mediation. Mediation is also used in business settings.

Note: The mediator does not decide the case for the disputants. He acts as a facilitator. If the parties reach an agreement, the mediator writes it down. It is called a "settlement," or "mediated agreement," or "settlement at mediation," or—well, you get the idea! One could always mediate to decide what to call the agreement!

5. Arbitration: Occurs when, as in mediation, the parties use a neutral third person, an arbitrator. However, the arbitrator's role is quite different from that of a mediator. The arbitrator is chosen by both parties from a list of persons provided by government or private agencies. He hears both sides present their evidence in a setting that is somewhat like a court, but less formal and usually takes less time than a full trial. Then the arbitrator *makes* the decision for the parties, specifying their rights and responsibilities.

Note: This is very different from the mediator, who does not decide the parties' legal rights and responsibilities, but only facilitates their agreements.

Arbitration is often incorporated into

—labor contracts,
—business contracts,
—consumer laws such as automobile "lemon laws,"
—and contracts between parties. For example, in fee disputes between lawyers and their clients! "If we can't agree on a fee, we'll take this matter to binding arbitration."

In these cases the arbitrator's decision is almost always binding. That is, the parties agree to live with the decision and not to appeal it (except on rare occasions). In other cases, as when a judge orders parties to arbitration instead of pursuing their lawsuit, the arbitrator's decision may not be binding. (Remember: people cannot be deprived of their day in court, i.e., their *due process rights*!)

As you can see, even with Alternative Dispute Resolution there are several alternatives.

VERBS IN COURT: WHO DOES WHAT TO WHOM?

Legalese can be obscure because lawyers often use common words in very specific ways. When a lawyer "moves," he doesn't take his furniture. A judge who "renders a decision" is not rendering fat, as a cook does, or rendering a drawing, as an architect does. When a lawyer "examines" you, he's not checking you out as a doctor would, and when a judge "charges the jury," he's not buying something with plastic! And even though *quash* sounds like *squash,* it's not. So here goes: some common verbs as used by lawyers, judges, and you, when you're involved with them in court.

The witness may:

1. Testify: In court (or administrative hearing or deposition or other judicial or quasi-judicial settings), you don't "speak" or "answer"! You testify: that is, you answer questions under oath; you give testimony (evidence) to the court.

Oath: A pledge to tell the truth. For those who refuse to take an oath, an affirmation will do. It affirms (states) that the person will tell the truth. Perjury, the crime of lying under oath, is taken *very* seriously by judges and is a felony.

2. Depose: Answer questions under oath before a trial, transcribed by a court reporter. This testimony creates a document, called the deposition; the witness is the deponent.

"The witness was deposed a month before trial at the lawyer's office." Depositions are part of pretrial discovery. (See page 145.) Watch this! If you are a deponent, be sure your testimony at trial is consistent with your testimony at the deposition. If it's not, it raises many troubling questions: Might it be perjury? An honest mistake? Is the witness believable (credible)? When was he telling the truth?—now? then? never?

3. Remain silent: Refuse to testify. A witness who may incriminate himself has the right to remain silent. This usually means the defendant (Δ) in a criminal proceeding or someone who may be charged with a crime because of the testimony.

The theory is: The Δ is innocent till proven guilty, and it is the government's job to convict him. He cannot be forced to help the government's case against him, i.e., incriminate himself.

Note: Only a witness who may incriminate himself has this privilege. Others, such as those with immunity (an exemption from prosecution in exchange for the witness's testimony) may not assert the privilege against self-incrimination. If such a witness refuses to testify, he may be cited for contempt. The court may punish a witness for disobeying the court or impairing the dignity of the court.

The lawyer(s) or litigant *pro se* (representing himself without a lawyer) may:

1. **Move:** Ask the court for something through a motion. The lawyer (for his client) then is called the movant, the moving party. "I move that . . ."

There are many types of motions. For example, a motion to change venue, a motion to quash, a motion to suppress evidence. Lawyers will tell you that the way these motions are dealt with by the court before the trial even begins often make or break their case. Motions are a vital part of what goes on in courts.

Lots of motions keep lots of lawyers very busy!

2. **Object:** Protest: The lawyer may argue against specific testimony or procedures. "I object!"

3. **Depose:** Same word as above. Here, the lawyer takes the deposition from the witness. "The lawyer deposed the witness."

4. **Examine:** Ask questions. There are two forms of examination: direct examination and cross-examination.

   (a) **Direct examine:** Ask questions of his own witness. The purpose is to present evidence favorable to the lawyer's client.

   (b) **Cross-examine:** Ask questions of a witness brought to court ("called") by the other side. The purpose is to discredit or clarify evidence to make it more favorable to the lawyer's client.

5. **Impeach the witness:** During cross-examination a lawyer may attempt to prove that the witness is not credible (a liar?) and should not be believed. This is called impeaching the witness.

6. **Rest his case:** Tell the court (the judge) that he's presented all his evidence and wants to end his presentation. He's finished. . . .

7. **Rebut:** Surprise! You thought it was all over, didn't you? Not so fast! The lawyer may present evidence to disprove facts presented by the other

side in some situations even after he rests. This happens especially if the other side presents facts that could not have been anticipated—surprises.

During the trial, the judge may:

1. **Quash:** Vacate, annul, make void. A motion to quash testimony, if approved, gets rid of it. "Motion to quash is granted." So the testimony is excluded or removed from the record.
2. **Sustain:** Approve, grant. "The judge granted—sustained—the plaintiff's (π's) motion." Yeah!
3. **Deny:** Refuse to grant. For example, "The judge denied the motion to quash." So the damaging evidence comes in.
4. **Order:** Direct, tell a party or the parties to do something during the course of the trial. For example, an order to show cause, or a temporary restraining order (TRO).

    There are lots of orders, which generally are not part of the final judgment. They are interlocutory: i.e., provisional, temporary, et cetera. (See **Legal Twosomes and Threesomes,** page 173.)
5. **Rule:** Make a decision on a legal question during the trial.
6. **Overrule:** Another word for deny.
7. **Adjourn:** Say good night, Judge! The judge may postpone the trial till the next day, next week, whenever.

At the end of a trial by jury the judge may:

8. **Charge the jury:** This occurs at the end of a jury trial. The charge is the judge's instructions to the jury, telling the members of the jury which laws

to apply to their verdict, which burden of proof must be met, and so on.

9. **Sequester the jury:** (Actually, a judge can do this both during and after the trial.) Separate the jury from their normal routines, often by having them stay in a hotel during the trial or during their deliberations. (See below.)

The jury may:

1. **Deliberate:** In the jury room. Discuss, consider, argue, ponder among themselves. Decide which witness to believe; which, if any, is not credible.
2. **Request clarification:** Ask the judge for more information, to see documents, to get clarification, et cetera.
3. **Return a verdict:** Make a decision. In criminal cases the verdict must be unanimous. In civil cases it depends on the state, the law that applies, the court, and so on.
4. **Not reach a verdict:** Become deadlocked, unable to decide for one side or the other. This is called a "hung jury."

    In such a case often a new trial may begin, and we go back to square one!

    Note: To hold a new trial in the case of a hung jury, even in a criminal case, would not be double jeopardy. (See page 126.)

After the trial without a jury the court (one or more judges) may:

1. **Render an opinion:** Write, deliver the judgment (decision).

2. **Affirm:** Decide—by an appellate court—that the lower court's decision in a particular case is right and should stand.

3. **Reverse:** Opposite of affirm. Set aside the lower court's decision. The appellate court's decision to vacate, annul, or change the lower court's decision in the same case. In this way our laws change; new laws and precedents are created.

4. **Vacate:** Cancel, annul. Another word for *reverse*.

5. **Remand:** Send back. An appellate court's decision to send a case back to the lower court where it was heard first, either for a new trial or for changes, as ordered by the appellate court.

6. **Hold:** Decide, declare, state. *The* important sentence or sentences in a decision that decide the case and can be used as precedent for other cases. Remember the Declaration of Independence? "We *hold* these truths . . ." Same word. "We hold that . . ." Lawyers read cases for the holdings.

7. **Overrule:** Annul, reverse, reject. An appellate court's ruling in a case that is directly opposite an earlier decision by a lower court in that jurisdiction. The second case may involve different parties, but the question of law may be the same as in the earlier case. Once a case is overruled, it no longer serves as precedence in that jurisdiction. Thus, too, do our laws evolve and change.

A famous overruling was *Brown* v. *Board of Education,* a 1954 case that found "separate but equal" schools inherently unequal (and a violation of the Constitution). This case overruled the 1896 case, *Plessy* v. *Ferguson,* which upheld laws permitting separate but equal facilities. Those laws were called "Jim Crow" laws.

LATIN,
JARGON . . .
LEGALESE!

LATIN POWER FOR FUN

. . . and to impress your friends (and lawyer)

Lawyers sometimes use Latin terms to explain (or is it to confuse?) and clarify (or muddle?) the law. For the client it's better to know these terms than to be always overwhelmed (or befuddled). Here is a starter sampling.

WHAT THE LAWYER SAYS	WHAT THE LATIN MEANS

Smith was caught vandalizing a car. Clearly, he was *in delicto*. His school had not supervised him enough, even though it was not acting *in loco parentis*. Smith could act *sui juris*, as he was not a minor.

He did not fight his case *pro se*, nor did a lawyer take his case on a *pro bono* basis. A lawyer was appointed for him, because Smith could not afford to hire one. Also, Smith did not have a *guardian ad litem*. He was not a ward. Since he was not *non compos mentis*, he was able to face the charges against him.

He knew that *"ignorantia legis non excusat,"* and that this was not a case of an *ex post facto* law.

In delicto: At fault, in the wrong.

In loco parentis: In the place of the parent, assuming the parent's obligations.

Sui juris: Of his own right, on his own.

Pro se: For himself, acting as his own lawyer.

Pro bono: For the good, a lawyer who represents someone without charging him. From the term *pro bono publico:* for the public good.

Guardian ad litem: Person appointed by a court to protect a ward's interests.

Non compos mentis: Not in control of his mind, or insane, or not legally competent.

Ignorantia legis non excusat: Ignorance of the law is no excuse. Just because someone doesn't know that an act is illegal does not prevent him from being *prosecuted* for doing that act. He could have/should have known.

Ex post facto law: After the fact. A law that punishes as a crime an act done when it was not considered crimi-

WHAT THE LAWYER SAYS	WHAT THE LATIN MEANS
	nal, or which imposes a stiffer penalty on an act after the fact. It's like changing the rules of the game in the middle. The *Constitution* prohibits these laws.
In fact, *ab initio,* he knew he had no good defense against the government's *prima facie* case. What to do?	*Ab initio:* From the beginning. *Prima facie* case: On its face. A case that will win unless the other side can produce strong evidence against it.
No one wrote an *amicus curiae* brief for him. (His case was so minor— *de minimis.*) Remember, *"De minimis non curat lex."*	*Amicus curiae:* Friend of the court. Someone not involved in the case who is interested in its outcome and writes a *brief* for the court. This brief gives information on questions of law and urges the court to reach a specific outcome. *De minimis:* Trifling, small matter. *De minimis non curat lex:* The law does not care about small matters. A court may throw out a case because of its insignificance.
Unfortunately for Smith, the court did not dismiss his case, *In re* Smith. Given all of the above Smith pleaded *nolo contendere.*	*In re:* In the matter of. The name of the case. *Nolo contendere:* I will not contest it. The defendant agrees to be punished, admits the facts of the case, but does not directly admit his guilt.

WHAT'S IN A NAME? SOMETIMES EVERYTHING!

When you are dealing with the law, you may be called a ——ee, an ——ant, or an ——or!

Which is which when?

Here are some common categories of people as they appear in legal situations.

1. Bailor and bailee

   The bailor delivers property to a bailee to hold and return later to the bailee.

   When I park my car in your garage and leave you the keys, I am the bailor; you are the bailee. The car is the bailment.

   If I don't leave the key, then I am the lessee and you are the lessor: I simply rent space from you.

   Who cares, you say! You do, if something happens to my car and I'm looking for someone to sue! It may be easier to sue a bailee than a lessor.

   Other everyday bailments: leaving valuables at the hotel desk; taking clothes to the cleaners; taking your car to the garage for a tune-up. (Remember, if the mechanic does the job, he now has a lien on your car that ends when you pay for the work. If you don't pay, guess who may own part of the car!)

2. Creditor and debtor and (sometimes) surety

   The debtor owes an obligation (often money) to the creditor. A surety guarantees the debtor's debt through a suretyship arrangement. "I promise to pay Dee's debt if he fails to do it."

   Here are some of the many everyday creditor/debtor relations.

   A. Mortgagor (home buyer, debtor) owes money to the mortgagee (often a bank, creditor).

   B. Borrower (debtor) owes money to the lender (creditor—often a bank).

   C. Obligor owes an obligation to the obligee.

   D. Promisor owes a promise to the promisee.

3. Donor and donee

The donor gives a gift to the donee. Nice and easy.

4. Drawer, drawee, and payee

In writing a check the drawer writes an order to the drawee (often the bank) to pay money to the payee. (See page 71.)

5. Employer, employee, and independent contractor

The employer hires the employee to work. Other terms for *employer* include *boss, owner, master*. Other terms for *employee* include *worker, servant*.

The terms *master* and *servant*, as used here, have specific legal meanings. A master employs someone and directs how the work is done, as well as the finished product. You own a painting company and hire painters. You instruct them in how to paint, what process to use, what materials to buy, et cetera.

A different relation exists between an employer and an independent contractor. In this case the employer directs the finished product only. "I want my house painted red." I don't tell you how to paint it. I pay when the house is painted.

Who cares? Again, you do, when it's time to pay employee taxes, sue for a job poorly done, or deal with a work-related injury, among other things.

In law so much depends on how you characterize someone! We move on. . . .

6. Garnishee, debtor, and creditor

Sometimes, in enforcing an order against a debtor, a court may use the process of garnishment. The court orders the garnishee (often, the employer) to pay a portion of the debtor's wages to creditors. In this way money held by a third party (the garnishee) may be attached for payment to a creditor. Laws limit the amount of wages that can be garnished. See state laws. (See page 142.)

7. Grantor and grantee

The grantor transfers an interest in real estate to the grantee. Often the grantor is the seller and the grantee is the buyer.

These folks may also be called the assignor (grantor) and the assignee (grantee).

8. Guardian and ward

The guardian (appointed by a court) has legal responsibility for the care of a ward (often a child or incompetent adult). The relationship between guardian and ward is called a "guardianship."

Related terms:

A. **Next friend:** Someone acting for another person, like a child, without a court appointment.

B. *Guardian ad litem:* Someone appointed by a court to advocate for a ward's interest in a particular court case (litigation). (See **Who Is a Person?,** page 16.)

9. Lessor and lessee

I always found these confusing!

The lessor is the landlord; lessee is the tenant. Why don't they just say so? Oh, well, it's better than calling them the "party of the first part" and the "party of the second part"! That happens too.

10. The plaintiff and defendant

The plaintiff (π) starts a lawsuit against a defendant (Δ). The π seeks a remedy from the Δ. These Greek letters are often used by lawyers for these terms.

11. Appellant and appellee

Whoever loses the lawsuit and appeals to a higher court is called the "appellant" (also called the "plaintiff in error." Sometimes, simply "a sore loser"). The former winner, now, in the appeals stage, is called the "appellee" (also called the "defendant in error" or respondent).

The appellant wants to reverse the lower court. The appellee wants to affirm the lower-court decision.

12. Settlor, trustee, and beneficiary

In making a trust the settlor (also called the trustor) creates a trust for the benefit of the beneficiary to be managed by the trustee.

A trust is one of the great legal inventions, an instrument that splits property into two forms of ownership: the legal and the equitable ownership.

The trustee has legal title to the trust property (called the corpus). The beneficiary has equitable title. In this case the equitable title is the valuable one! The trust eventually and actually belongs to him.

The relation between the trustee, the beneficiary, the settlor, and the trust is called a fiduciary relationship. In plain English, this means the trustee had better do a good job and serve the interests of those other folks, and not himself.

13. Vendor and vendee

The vendor is the seller. The vendee is the buyer.

LEGAL TWOSOMES AND THREESOMES

Yes and no. Black and white. Peanut butter and jelly. Come and go. This-'n'-that . . . Terms that go together.

Again, much of law depends on what something is called. Once you decide what something is, different laws apply with different consequences.

So you see, in law, as in life itself, what you call something (or someone) is very important.

Here are some common pairs or threesomes

1. VESTED RIGHTS AND INTERESTS AND CONTINGENT RIGHTS AND INTERESTS (ALSO CALLED EXECUTORY INTERESTS)

Vested: A fixed, accrued right. For example, damages you won in a trial. Money owed to you for work you have completed.

Contingent: A possible right or interest that is not fixed or actual, but depends on a future event or possibility that may happen. For example, damages you may win in a trial. The amount for which you are suing. Money you plan to earn in your new job.

If you're suing someone, all other things being equal, it's probably better to go after vested interests than contingent interests. That's following the (practical/nonlegal) principle of "a bird in the hand . . ."

Vested and contingent: These are the principles that underlie all law students' battle with the *Rule against Perpetuities.* (Is it because they finally got through this Rule that lawyers charge so much?) That Rule, by the way, states that contingent interests in property must vest not later than twenty-one years after some specific life in being (or in gestation—that is, the nine months of pregnancy. They thought of everything, did they not!). The Rule is designed to free up property and not permit unreasonable restraints on property to tie it up for years and years, generation after generation.

A fun rule to bring up at your next cocktail party with your lawyer! So much for vested and contingent interests. . . .

2. DOMICILE AND RESIDENCE

Domicile: A person's permanent home, principal residence. It's where you vote, write your will, usually pay your taxes. A person may have only one domicile, but many residences.

Residence: A person's home. It may be permanent or temporary. A person may have many residences, often depending on how rich he is or how many suitcases he likes to pack. A vacation home is usually a residence, not a domicile.

Many rights and responsibilities flow from whether that house is your residence or domicile or you're just passing through.

3. TANGIBLE AND INTANGIBLE PROPERTY

Tangible: Something you can hold, possess, whether it's real estate or personal property. For example, your house, car, jewels, lawn mower.

Intangible: Something that is evidence of property, but not the real thing! It's—ready?—incorporeal. For example, a copyright, easement, or franchise.

4. TANGIBLE AND INCHOATE

Tangible: Complete, vested.

Inchoate: Imperfect, begun, incomplete. For example, an inchoate instrument (document) is one that must be registered but isn't yet, such as a deed. Before it is registered, it's inchoate, valid only between the two parties. After it's registered, it's valid against the whole world: everyone is assumed to have notice of it.

5. MANIFEST, PATENT, AND LATENT

Patent/Manifest: Obvious. Can be seen by normal inspection. For example, when selling your home, you leave all the defects, such as water damage in the basement, for all potential buyers to see. It may be hard for one of them to sue you later because there is water damage in the basement. He knew or should have known about that patent/manifest defect.

Latent: Hidden, not obvious. Can't be seen by normal inspection. For example, when buying a car, you do the usual inspection (look under the hood, drive it around, have a mechanic check it over). However, the car turns out to have a defect in the engine that could only be discovered by taking the engine apart. You may have an easier time suing the seller because of this latent defect than you would if suing over a patent defect.

In tort law, often the defendant's (Δ's) negligence depends on whether the defect was latent or patent.

6. EXPRESS AND IMPLIED

Express: Unmistakable, clear, specified.

Implied: Intended, but not expressed in words. Implied from action or inaction.

An express consent is definite and clear. "I agree to . . ." An implied consent may be assumed from my behavior. It is said that driving is a privilege. If I get a license, I am deemed to have implied to consent to obey the rules of the road. This is why, if I refuse a Breathalyzer test, in many states the police may take my license—even if I'm not guilty of driving under the influence. I had consented to that test. (This law is being closely watched and tested in many jurisdictions at this time.)

These terms are also important in waivers and warranties. Different consequences flow from each, whether express or implied.

7. SOLVENT AND BANKRUPT

Solvent: Your money and assets exceed your obligations (debts). You have enough money and other assets (things you own) to pay your bills.

Bankrupt: Your debts (obligations) exceed your assets. All the money and assets you own are not enough to pay your bills as they become due. You can't pay your bills and all your creditors are after you. To declare yourself bankrupt, in order to gain protection from creditors or to reorganize your affairs, you have to proceed through Bankruptcy Court.

8. *NISI* AND ABSOLUTE

Nisi: "Unless." Something will happen *unless* something else occurs. For example, a divorce decree *nisi* will be finalized after a specified time *unless* someone shows that it should not be made absolute.

Also called "interlocutory." For example, an interlocutory divorce decree.

Absolute: Final, complete.

9. COERCED AND VOLUNTARY

Coerced: Forced to do something under duress, compulsion. Forced to obey against one's will. This will often invalidate an action.

Voluntary: Completely free of coercion. Assurance to this effect is often required to validate the action. For example, a waiver must be knowing and voluntary, in order to be effective.

These terms are important in wills, in issues of consent, and in criminal confessions, for example. We all know that a will that is proven to have been coerced may be invalid. The same goes for a confession or consent.

10. CONSTRUCTIVE AND REAL

Constructive: Not actual, not real, but accepted legally as if it were. For example, constructive eviction: If a tenant abandons a property that the landlord made uninhabitable (as by turning off the heat and water), then, even though the landlord didn't actually throw the tenant out, his actions have done so constructively.

There are also such things as constructive trust, constructive notice, constructive delivery. *Constructive possession:* In this case you have the power to own the property, but you're not there.

Real: Actual, factual, real. For example, an actual eviction (unlike a constructive eviction): "You are hereby notified that after December thirty-first, your lease will not be renewed" . . . or some similar language. *Real, actual possession* (unlike constructive possession): In this case you are actually on the property or have the property in question.

When does it matter? For example, in a criminal case, the driver of a car carrying weapons or drugs in the trunk may argue that he was not in possession of that contraband. In contrast, the prosecution may argue that he was, as he had the keys (the power over the property).

And so it goes. . . . What you call something is vitally important in law, as in life!

JARGON: LAWYERS' SHOPTALK

Lawyers, like other professionals and athletes, have their own language. Shoptalk. Jargon. Sometimes this jargon may be off putting—mysterious.

From "apples" to "hands," "fruit" to "fishing," "black" to "blue," here are examples of common words with uncommon and precise legalistic meaning.

1. TWO BITES AT THE APPLE

    Generally not permitted. It's the idea that someone will have more than one chance to argue his case before a court; to present his evidence more than once.

    In law you get one try! Be prepared to give it your best shot!

2. FORUM SHOPPING

    Supposedly not permitted. This occurs when a litigant or defendant (Δ) tries to have his case heard in a particular court by a particular judge—where he thinks the outcome may be better.

3. FRUIT-OF-THE-POISONOUS-TREE DOCTRINE

    Constitutionally based. Evidence that is obtained through an illegal search or seizure or illegal interrogation is "fruit of the poisonous tree" and may generally not be used as evidence against a Δ. For example, a gun is illegally seized by the police. The number on the gun may not be used to identify the owner. This doctrine has evolved over the years to respond to the Fourth Amendment rule against unreasonable searches and seizures without properly obtained warrants.

4. CLEAN HANDS

   The equity doctrine that the court will not grant relief to a person who acted wrongfully (had unclean hands) when he complains of someone else's wrongdoing.

5. FISHING EXPEDITION

   A discovery technique, whereby a party seeks to get information from the other side by asking questions in a general and vague manner. Also, courtroom questions that are vague and broadly phrased, trying to pull in all sorts of material, like a fishing net. Courts may limit the scope of such discovery through protective orders and by disallowing such questions at trial.

6. FIRST IMPRESSION

   A case that presents the court with a new question of law, so that there may be no precedents on which the court may rely to reach its decision.

7. ARM'S-LENGTH TRANSACTION

   A deal negotiated by parties who are unrelated by blood, marriage, ownership, or other relationship, where each party may be said to act in his/her/its own self-interest. When related parties negotiate deals, they need to meet this standard in order for the deal to be considered a reflection of a fair market value. For example, in tax situations, when a value is placed on property, its price needs to have been reached at "arm's length."

8. MEETING OF THE MINDS

Hard to picture, isn't it! But it's what lawyers call the manifestation, or demonstration, of the mutual agreement necessary to form a contract (K). To be enforceable, a K reflects the parties' mutual intent as demonstrated by their acts and deeds at the time.

9. RIPENESS DOCTRINE

Has nothing to do with fruit. This is a constitutional doctrine. Courts will not decide cases before they have matured, before there is a concrete controversy that must be adjudicated. Courts do not deal with hypothetical cases or with parties who do not have an actual interest in the outcome of the case. It's not enough to have a dispute that may be interesting or socially important. Also, if the dispute has vanished or been resolved (gone beyond ripe!), courts won't hear it. Then we're into the mootness doctrine.

Now for some color words!

Black
  Black letter law: Basic legal principles, usually accepted by judges and lawyers. The roots. The foundation.
  Blacklist: Illegal. A list of persons whom the lister

wishes to single out for ostracism, boycott, avoidance, negative publicity. It was used by employers against certain workers who participated in legal union activities; by businesses listing persons who are bad credit risks, insolvent, et cetera.

Blackmail: A crime, a form of extortion. Threatening to harm a person or his property, to accuse him of a crime, to expose damaging information about the person (even if true), or to use other similar threats in order to demand (extort) money.

Black market: Buying, trading, and selling goods and services "under the table," illegally, without declaring any income on the transactions—and without paying any taxes on them. Or, buying, trading, and selling goods that are illegal—contraband.

Blue

Blue chip stocks: Stocks that generally are considered to be less risky than other stocks. They are considered to be safer investments because they represent old, well-known, and well-established companies. Initially, the stocks may have sold at a hundred dollars per share—like the casino's blue chips! Thus, the name.

Blue laws: Local or state laws that mandate the closing of certain businesses on Sunday.

Blue sky laws: State regulations of the sale of stocks. Designed to protect citizens from fraudulent companies.

Red

Red herring: In a legal argument, an issue raised that is interesting and possibly important—but has no relevance at all to the issues of the case. It's a diversionary tactic.

Also, a prospectus sent to the SEC (Securities and

Exchange Commission) before a stock issue. It may be copied in red—for information only!

Redlining: Unlawful as discriminatory. It's a way to limit credit to homeowners based in certain neighborhoods. It does not take into account the creditworthiness of the specific potential property owner.

Redlining used to show up on city maps—in red, often singling out minority neighborhoods.

White

White-collar crime: Nonviolent crimes committed by corporations, businesses, executives, public officials, and management types—all sorts of people who wear white-collared shirts and suits (as distinguished from violent street crimes; sometimes called "blue-collar crime"). These crimes may involve corruption, fraud, bribery, extortion, and other commercial crimes.

HAVING TO DO WITH . . .

In legalese lots of adjectives can throw you. Don't let them. Here are some words that "have to do with" . . . something. These are big words that are easy to cut down to size.

Conjugal
Matrimonial
Marital   —————— have to do with marriage.
Nuptial

Domiciliary	has to do with domicile (where you have your principal home).
Evidentiary	has to do with evidence.
Natal	has to do with birth (prenatal, neonatal, postnatal).
Pecuniary	has to do with money.
Penal	has to do with punishment (penalty, penalty box, penalize).
Personalty	has to do with personal property.
Proprietary	has to do with ownership.
Punitive	has to do with punishment.
Realty	has to do with real estate (real property).
Testamentary	has to do with a will.

PRACTICAL
LEGALESE

HOW TO FIND A LAWYER

(aka Attorney, Counselor)

Finding the right lawyer may be intimidating. If you are the client in search of the lawyer, remember—YOU are hiring HIM. He, not you, is interviewing for the job. This fact may help set your mind at ease as you begin the search.

Lawyer: A person licensed to practice law. He is hired *(retained)* by you, the client, to work on your behalf and represent your interest in all types of legal matters.

A possible route to follow to find an appropriate attorney:

1. Identify your legal needs. What type of matter is it: criminal? tax? divorce? personal injury (accident)? malpractice? a business deal? buying/selling a home? *Legalese* may help you sort out these areas of law.

2. Decide if you need a lawyer. You may or may not. For example, if it's a small money matter, you may be better off going to *small claims court* without a lawyer. (See page 148.) If it's a tax matter, perhaps an accountant or tax planner will be more helpful.

3. Once you decide you need a lawyer, try to head straight for the one who can handle your needs.

Note: Some lawyers specialize in specific areas of law (such as those noted above), while others have a "general practice," handling all sorts of cases. You'll have to decide which type is right for you.

4. Make a list of possible attorneys. Here are some steps you may take in this search:

- —Ask around for recommendations from friends, family, an attorney you used on another matter, colleagues at work, church acquaintances, and so on.
- —Call the local *bar association* or lawyer referral agency. These groups list lawyers who ask to be listed. A referral is not a recommendation but may be a helpful starting place. (See phone book's yellow pages under "Lawyers.")
- —Check lawyer directories at the public library. The most widely known is the *Martindale Hubbell Law Directory,* a who's who of lawyers. It lists all attorneys and law firms in a state (by city) and provides basic information about each lawyer: including age, law school attended, year of admission to the bar, et cetera.
- —Call a chapter of local public interest or special-interest groups that deal with your area of legal needs. They may maintain a list of lawyers who practice in the field for which you need a lawyer.
- —Check with your employer if you are entitled to use a *prepaid legal plan*.
- —If you qualify (by having a low income) find out about free or low-cost legal services in your community.
- —If your situation involves a specific government agency, call that agency for names of lawyers who practice in that specialty. Examples include immigration, tax, and bankruptcy matters. It is worth noting that government agencies are an excellent source of information about procedures, rights, time lines, and so on. Also, the clerk of the

court where your case may be may provide information ("technical assistance") to the public.

—If you live near a law school, check if there is a legal clinic. Most have one! Often, law students provide legal services at low cost to the public.

The above suggestions should lead to your coming up with a list of possible attorneys.

5. Call the lawyer.

In this initial phone call state your needs, determine whether the attorney practices in that field, ask if he will see you for an initial office conference and whether that consultation is free or what it will cost, and make that appointment, if appropriate.

Your antennae should be up! Are you treated with respect? Can the lawyer see you soon? Does he put you off for a month? Does he have too much time available? Too little? You should get a sense of how the office operates and whether you feel comfortable there.

6. Attend the initial office conference well prepared.

The main goal of this meeting is for you to decide whether to retain this attorney. Come well prepared with a written summary of the facts in your case, the documents you have, a possible list of witnesses, et cetera. A written chronology is often useful. Listen carefully to the lawyer's reactions to your case. You may wish to take notes.

Ask questions about his prior experience in this field, the likelihood of success, how long the matter should take, fees; also ask who will be doing the work. Will it be the lawyer you interviewed or will it be delegated to an

associate—a younger, less experienced lawyer, or
paralegal—a nonlawyer trained to do routine matters.

7. You may wish to have an initial office conference with another attorney.

8. Following all the initial conferences you have, decide which attorney to retain.

Always remember, it is *you* who are hiring the attorney—not the other way around!

See the following pages for a discussion of lawyer fees and expenses. Once you decide to retain a lawyer, there should be a contract, specifying the terms of his employment, your rights and responsibilities, fees, and other details.

THE BOTTOM LINE

Fees and costs of legal services

When a client "buys" legal services, he hires/*retains* the lawyer for a fee. Generally, the fee is for the lawyer's time and advice. Some of these services include consultations, research, letter writing, telephoning, and meeting with opposing counsel.

Below is a primer of the legalese a client needs to know in order to understand various billing practices.

Items on legal bills are in two basic categories: *fees* and *costs/expenses*. *Fees* are payments for the lawyer's time and services rendered. *Costs/expenses* are for all other items and services involved in the client's matter. Both of these are explained below.

The three basic *fee* arrangements are:

Hourly fee: The client pays for the lawyer's services by the hour or other unit of time.

Some lawyers break the time down into minimum billing units (mbu); e.g., one quarter hour or one tenth of an hour. For example, if a client pays a hundred dollars per hour, then a five-minute phone call would cost twenty-five dollars with a 15-minute mbu, and ten dollars with a six-minute mbu.

Lawyers may charge different fee rates for different members of their office who work on a legal matter. Thus the lead attorney's rate may be higher than an associate's or a paralegal's.

Contingency Fee: This fee structure is used most often in cases where a client may not be able to afford the legal services if he loses a case. That is, the payment for the legal services may come from the winnings. Thus, the contingency! These cases often include collections and personal injury cases, or torts. If the case is won or settled favorably, the lawyer will receive a percentage of the amount the client receives in court or through a settlement. The percentage may vary between twenty-five and fifty percent; usually, it is around thirty-three percent.

By this fee structure both the lawyer and client assume the risk of failure. Presumably, they may be unlikely to pursue a case that is frivolous (has little chance of winning). That, at least, is the theory of these fee structures! As you undoubtedly know if you keep up with the news, they are controversial. Do they encourage litigation? Are lawyers earning too much? Too little? Do they make it possible for the "little guy" to obtain top-notch legal services?

Within the contingency fee arrangement, fees are calculated in many ways. Often there is a sliding scale, depending on how far the case is argued in court or whether it is settled before a trial or whether there is an appeal of the trial court verdict or decision.

In most cases, win or lose, the client will pay the expenses of the case. Again, as with all agreements and contracts, these matters are subject to negotiation between the attorney and client.

Fixed Fee: The client pays an agreed-upon amount for the service, such as writing a will, getting a divorce, incorporating a business, et cetera. Usually, these fees are used for matters that are routine. The lawyer-client agreement may specify that if the matter gets more complicated, then fees will be adjusted upward. A related fee structure is the annual retainer. This structure is often used by businesses or other entities that have ongoing needs for legal services. By this arrangement the client hires, or retains, the attorney for the year (or whatever time period is agreed upon) at a certain rate. Then, whatever legal issues emerge, the attorney's fees have already been accounted for. As part of this arrangement the lawyer and client may agree that certain costs over a specified minimum be billed differently, as on an hourly fee basis.

Other fee arrangements: There are statutory fees in certain areas of the law. (For example, in workmen's compensation cases.) Check the laws.

Sometimes lawyers will work on a case for free—as a *pro bono* matter. This term means "for the good." Lawyers are encouraged to take cases on this basis as part of their public service obligation. Often nonprofit and charitable organizations have *pro bono* lawyers.

Indigent (poor) criminal defendants (Δ's) have a constitutional right to the "assistance of counsel" regardless of their ability to pay (Sixth Amendment). States have *public defenders* who serve these clients. Check local laws for the various arrangements.

Expenses/costs: These are for services and items over and above the lawyer's *fees*. The client usually pays for the costs of his case, no matter which fee structure is used or whether he succeeds or not.

The expenses may include the following:

1. Filing fee: Payment to the court for the right to sue there. Yes, we pay for the privilege of using the courts!

2. Deposition fee (see page 158): Fees may include witness fees, stenographer, transcripts, et cetera.

3. Subpoena fee: These are the costs of bringing a person to court whose testimony is required. The payment is to the person who "serves" the witness, or *party* being sued. The subpoena gives notice of the suit to the Δ; or, to the witness, notice of his need to appear in court. Called "service of process." Client pays!

4. Expert Witness Fee (see page 130): Fees are for the witness's time in court, preparation time, travel expenses, and so on.

5. Expenses for any of the following:

—long-distance phone calls, fax
—photocopying of long documents
—postage, messenger service
—document searches
—research and investigation (for example, the use of a private detective)
—other incidentals

Costs and fees should be understood by the client; they should be discussed and appear in the contract.

6. Costs to the prevailing (winning) *party*. In some cases—by statute—the loser pays the winner's costs—in certain types of cases. Check the relevant statutes.

EPILOGUE

Now you're ready to see a lawyer. You can make sense of the language of law.

INDEX

Abandonment, 86
Abatement, 85
Ab initio, 168
Absolute, 177
Acceptance (of a contract), 42
Accord and satisfaction, 47
Adjourn, 161
Administrative law, 100
  judges, 100
Administrator/-trix, 55
Adoptive parents, 22
Affidavit, 132–53
Affirm, 163
Age
  of majority, 19
  of minority, 19
Alimony, 51–52
Alternative dispute resolution
    (ADR), 155–57
Amicus curiae, 168
Annulment, 50
Answer, 152
Appeal, 147
Appellant/appellee, 172
Appellate jurisdiction, 99
Arbitration, 156–57
Armed robbery, 120
"Arm's-length transaction,"
    180–81

Arrest warrant, 153
Artificial condition, 33
Assault, 34
Assignment, 86
Associate, 189
Audit, 67
Automatic extension (taxes), 65

Bailiff, 130
Bailor/bailee, 169
Bankrupt, 176–77
Bar, 131
  association, 188
Bargain and sale deed, 81
Battery, 34
Bench warrant, 153
Beneficiary, 54, 172
Bequest, 56
Beyond a reasonable doubt, 101
Bill, 133
Black
  letter law, 181
  market, 182
Blacklist, 181–82
Blackmail, 182
Blue
  chip stocks, 182
  laws, 182
  sky laws, 182

Bond, 55
Breach, 46
   of duty, 69
Breaking and entering, 120
Burden of proof, 101
Burglary, 120
By a preponderance of the
      evidence, 102

Canon, 15
Capital
   gains income, 64
   punishment, 124
Causation, 31
   malpractice and, 69–70
Cease and desist order, 91
Certificate, 133
Change of venue, 100
Character witness, 129
Charge the jury, 161–62
Charter, 133
Checks, 71–73
Child custody, 52
Children, 18–24, 52–53
Child support, 52–53
Citations, 15–16
Civil case, basic procedure, 142–
      47
Civil laws, 9–11
   criminal laws and, 9–11
Class action lawsuit, 144
"Clean hands," 180
Clerk, 130
Closing, 81
Code, 14
Codicil, 58
Coerced, 177
Commission (real estate), 76–77
Common law, 12–13
   marriage, 48
   separate property and, 53
Community
   property, 53, 76
   service, 88
Commutation of sentence, 125

Comparative negligence, 113–14
Compensatory/actual damages,
      89
Competent persons, 18–19
Conciliation, 155
Concurrent jurisdiction, 98–99
Condominium, 74–75
Confinement, 88
Conflicts, 12
Conjugal, 183
Consent defense, 114
Conservator, 23
Consideration, 43
   in real estate, 82
Consortium, 48
   loss of, 89
Constitution(s), 11–12
   state, 12
   United States, 92
Constructive, 177
   eviction, 87
   notice, 82
Contempt
   of court, 49
   order, 146
Contested divorce, 51
Contingency fee, 191–92
Contingent rights and interests,
      173–74
Contraband, 154
Contract(s), 39–47, 133
   defined, 39–40, 43–44
   statute of limitations and, 104
Contributory negligence, 113
Conversion, 35
Cooperative (real estate), 75
Copyright, 104
Corporal punishment, 124
Corporations, 16–17
Counteroffer, 42
Countersuit, 144
Covenant, 85
   of habitability, 85
   of quiet enjoyment, 85
Creditor, 169–70, 171

Credits, 63
Criminal case, basic procedure, 136–42
Criminal homicide, 123
  chart, 118
Criminal laws, 9–11
  civil laws and, 9–11
Cross claim, 144
Cross-examine, 160
"Cruel and unusual punishment," 126
Curtesy, 56
Custodian, 55
Custody of children, 52

Damages, 88–90
  compensatory/actual, 89
  double (or treble), 89
  expectancy, 89–90
  mitigation of, 90
  nominal, 89
  punitive/exemplary, 89
Death tax, 59
Debtor, 169–70, 171
Decedent, 54
Deceit, 36
Decree, 134
Decree nisi, 53–54
Deductions, 62
Deed, 81–83, 134
  bargain and sale, 81
Defamation, 37
Default
  divorce, 51
  judgment, 152
Defendant, 129, 172
Defense(s), 112–14
  of property, 112
Deliberation, 162
De minimis, 99, 168
  non curat lex, 168
Deny, 161
Deposition, 145
  to depose, 158–59, 160
  fee, 193

Deputy sheriff, 131
Desertion, 49–50
Determinate sentence, 124
Devise, 56
Direct examination, 160
Directed verdict, 147
Discovery, 145
Disinherit, 57
Dispossession, 86
Dissolution of marriage, 50, 51
Diversity jurisdiction, 95, 96
Division of property, 53
Divorce and marriage, 48–54
  divorce decree, 53
Doctor's defenses, 70
Doctrine, 14
Domicile, 57, 174
Domiciliary, 184
Donor/donee, 170
Double
  jeopardy, 126
  (or treble) damages, 89
Dower and curtesy, 56
Drawer/drawee, 170
Durable power of attorney, 24
Duress defense, 113
Duty, 29
  of due care, 68–69
Earning capacity, loss of, 89
Easement, 79
Elect against the will, 56
Emancipation, 21–22
Embezzlement, 120
Employer/employee, 170
Encumbrance, 78
Enforceable, 45
Entrapment, 113
Equitable distribution, 53
Equity, 5–8
  courts, 6–8
Escheat, 59
Estate, 56
  tax, 59, 67
Eviction, 86
  constructive, 87

Evidentiary, 184
Examine a witness, 160
Exclusive (real estate), 77
Excusable homicide, 123
Executor/-trix, 55
Exemption, 62
Ex parte, 91
Expectancy damages, 89–90
Expenses, 193
Expert witness, 130
    fee, 193
Ex post facto, 105, 106, 167–68
Express consent, 176
Extortion, 120

Facts, 99
False imprisonment, 34–35
Fault divorce, 50
Federal jurisdiction, 95–96, 96–97
Federal questions, 96
Fee(s), 190–93
    real estate, 73
Fee simple, 74
    absolute, 74
    conditional, 74
Felonies, 117–19
Filing fee, 193
Filing status (taxes), 64
Final decree, 54
Financing (real estate), 80
Fine, 88, 124
"First impression," 180
"Fishing expedition," 180
Fixed fee, 192
Forgery, 73
    of checks, 73
"Forum shopping," 179
Foster parents, 23
"Fruit-of-the-poisonous-tree
        doctrine," 179–80
Full covenant and warranty deed,
    81
Full faith and credit, 107

Garnishee, 170–71

Gift, 44, 55
    tax, 67–68
Good Samaritan statutes, 30
Graduated tax, 64–65
Grandparent, 23
Granting language, 82
Grantor/grantee, 171
Gross income, 61
    adjusted, 62
Guardian, 23, 55, 171
Guardian ad litem, 167, 171

Habendum clause, 82
Harm
    to economic interests, 36–37
    to intangible property inter-
        ests, 37
Head of household (taxes), 64
Hearing
    examiners, 100, 132
    officers, 100, 132
Heir/heiress, 54–55
Hierarchical system of laws, 11–
    12
Hold, 163
Homicide, 122–23
    criminal (chart), 118
Hostile witness, 130
Hourly fee, 191
Hung jury, 126

Ignorantia legis non excusat, 167
Illegitimate children, 17
Immunity, 104, 114
Impeach the witness, 160
Implied consent, 176
Imprisonment, 124
    false, 34–35
Incarceration, 124
Inchoate, 175
Income
    adjustments to, 61–62
    capital gains, 64
    defined, 60–61
    gross, 61

net, 63
ordinary, 64
Incompetent persons, 18–19
In delicto, 167
Independent contractor, 170
Indeterminate sentence, 124
Indictment, 134
Infancy defense, 112
Inherit, 56
Inheritance tax, 59, 67
Injunction, 90
In loco parentis, 167
In personam jurisdiction, 95–96
In re, 168
Insanity defense, 112
Inspection (real estate), 80
Intangible property, 175
Intent, 4
wills and, 59
Intentional
harm to persons, 34–35
harm to property, 35
interference with advantageous
relations, 37
mental distress, 35
Interference with contractual
relationships, 37
Interlocutory decree, 53–54
Internal Revenue Code (IRC), 60
Internal Revenue Service (IRS),
61
Interrogatories, 134, 145
Interstate, 59
Intoxication defense, 113
Invasion of privacy, 37–38
Invitee, 32
Issue, 55

Joint
and several liability, 84
tenancy with right of survivorship, 75
Judge, 130
Judgment n.o.v. (*non obstante
veredicto*), 147

Jurisdiction, 13, 95
appellate, 99
concurrent, 98–99
federal, 95–96, 96–97
state, 96, 97–98
Jurisdictional amount, 96
Jury, 130–31
hung, 126
Justifiable homicide, 122
Juveniles, 18–24

Laches, 5, 105
statute of limitations and, 105
Landlord and tenant law, 83–87
Larceny, 119–21
by false pretenses, 72, 120–21
grand, 119
petty, 119
Latent, 175–76
Law, 99
administrative, 100
clerk, 130
Law courts, 7
equity courts and, 6–8
Lawyer(s), 131, 187–93
Lay witness, 130
Leading case, 13
Lease, 79–80, 83
Leased property, 84
Legacy, 56, 57
Legal
separation, 49
twosomes and threesomes, 32,
173–78
Lessor/lessee, 171
Libel, 37
License, 134
Licensee, 32–33
Lien, 78
tax, 68
Life estate, 74
Living together, 49
Loss
of consortium, 89
of earning capacity, 89

Lying by, 3

Magistrate, 131
Malicious prosecution, 37
Malpractice, 68–70
Manifest, 175
Marital, 183
Marriage and divorce, 48–54
Martindale Hubbell Law Directory, 188
Master and servant, 170
Material witness, 130
Matrimonial, 183
Mediation, 156
"Meeting of the minds," 181
Mens rea, 108
Mental
  capacity (wills), 57–58
  incompetency, 19
Minors, 18–24
Misdemeanors, 117–19
Misrepresentation, 121
Mistake of fact, 112
  and larceny, 121
Mitigation of damages, 90
Motion, 134, 159–60
  to dismiss, 101–02
Multiple listing service (MLS), 77–78

Natal, 184
Negligence, 28–33
  comparative, 113–14
  contributory, 113
Negligent misrepresentation, 36
Negotiation, 155
Net income, 63
Next friend, 23–24, 171
Next of kin, 55
Nisi, 77
No-fault divorce, 51
Nolo contendere, 168
Nominal damages, 89
Non compos mentis, 167
Notary, 82
Not reach a verdict, 162

Nuisance, 36
Null and void ab initio, 45
Nunc pro tunc, 106
Nuptial, 183

Oath, 158
Objection, 160
Offer, 41–42
Open listing, 77
Order, 134, 161
Ordinance, 135
Ordinary income, 64
Overdraft, 72
Overrule, 161, 163
Pain and suffering, 89
Palimony, 49, 51, 52
Paralegal, 189
Pardon, 125
Parens patriae, 21
Parents, 22–24
Parole, 124, 125
Parties, 129
Patents, 104, 175
Payee, 170
Pecuniary, 184
Penal, 184
Performance, 45
  specific, 47, 91
Periodic tenancy, 84
Personally, 184
Persons, defined, 16–24
Physical examination of a witness, 145
Pickpocketing, 120
Pilferage, 120
Plaintiff, 129, 172
Possession, 4
Power of attorney, 24
Prenuptial agreement, 48–49
Prepaid legal plan, 188
Pretrial conference, 146, 155–56
Prima facie case, 101, 168
Privilege, 114
Probable cause, 153
Probate, 58
Probation, 125

Pro bono, 167, 192
    publico, 167
Product liability, 33
Progressive tax, 65
Promissory estoppel, 44–45
Proof of Service, 152
Proprietary, 184
Pro se, 159, 167
Prosecuting attorney, 131
Prosecution, 129
Proving a will, 58
Public defenders, 192
Punishment, 87–88, 123–26
    capital, 124
    corporal, 124
    "cruel and unusual," 126
Punitive, 184
    (exemplary) damages, 89
Purse snatching, 120

Quantum meruit, 7
Quash, 161
Quickie divorce, 51
Quid pro quo, 43
Quitclaim deed, 81

Real, 177–78
Real estate broker, 76–78
    listing agreements, 77–78
Real estate law, 73–83
    brokers and, 76–78
    closing and deed, 81–83
    purchase and sale agreement,
        78–80
Realty, 184
Reasonable conduct, 29–30
Reasonable doubt, 101
Rebut, 160–61
Receipt of stolen property, 121
Record, 135
Recording (deeds), 82
Red herring, 183
Redlining, 183
Reformation, 91
Regressive tax, 65
Regulations, 14

Rejection, 42
Remain silent, 159
Remand, 163
Remedies, 46–47, 87–91
    in civil cases, 88–90
    in criminal cases, 87–88
    in equity cases, 90–91
Rendering an opinion, 162
Rent, 84
    strike, 85–86
Repair and deduct, 85
Reprieve, 125–26
Request
    for admissions, 145–46
    clarification
    for production, 145
Rescission, 46–47
Residence, 174
Res ipsa loquitur, 33
Rest a case, 160
Restitution, 47, 88, 90, 124
Retaliatory, 87
Retroactivity, 105–06
Return a verdict, 162
Reverse, 163
Revocation, 58
Riparian rights, 79
"Ripeness doctrine," 181
Robbery, 119–20
    armed, 120
Rule, 161
Rule against Perpetuities, 174
Rule 23 of Civil Procedure, 144–
        45
Sanctions, 146
Search warrant, 153
Self-defense, 112
Self-help, 87
Self-proving will, 58
Separation, 49
    legal, 49
Sequester a jury, 162
Servant, 170
Service of process, 151
Settlement, 146
Settlor, 172

Severalty tenancy, 75
Sheriff, 131
  deputy, 131
Shoplifting, 120
Signatures (deeds), 82
Slander, 37
Small claims court, 148–50
Sole tenancy, 75
Solvent, 176
Specific performance, 47, 91
Stale check, 73
Standard of proof, 10, 33, 101–02
Stare decisis, 13
State jurisdiction, 96, 97–98
States of mind (chart), 109–11
Status quo ante, 46
Statute, 135
Statute of limitations, 5, 103–05
  criminal cases, 104
  taxes and, 66–67
  tolling and, 103
Statutory
  laws, 13–14
  rape, 19–20
Stepparent, 22–23
Strict liability, 35–36
Sublet, 86
Subpoena, 135, 152–53
  fee, 193
Subpoena ad testificandum, 135
Subpoena duces tecum, 135, 153
Sui juris, 167
Summary
  judgment, 146
  process, 86
Summons, 135, 151–52
  and complaint, 151
Surrogate parent, 23
Suspended sentence, 125
Sustain, 161

Tangible property, 175
Tax(es), 60–68
  court, 67
  defined, 60
  individual, 60–67

lien, 68
penalties, 66
return, 61
statute of limitations and, 104–05
Temporary restraining order (TRO), 91
Tenancy, 75–76, 83–87
  by the entirety with right of survivorship, 76
  in common, 76
  joint, with right of survivorship, 75
  periodic, 84
  in severalty, 75
  sole, 75
  at sufferance, 84
  at will, 84
  for years, 84
1040 Form, 61
Term, 84
Testament, 135
Testamentary, 184
Testator/textatrix, 54
Testify, 158
Third-party complaint, 144
Time, 102–06
  retroactivity, 105–06
  statute of limitations, 103–05
Tolling, 103
Tort(s), 27–38
  defined, 27
  statute of limitations and, 103–04
  types of, 28–38
Traffic infractions, 117
Transfer tax, 59
Trespass
  to chattels, 35
  to land, 35
Trespasser, 33
Trial, 146–47
  courts, 99
Trustee, 172
Truth defense, 113
"Two bites at the apple," 179

Ultrahazardous activity, 36
Unborn children, 17–18
Uncontested divorce, 51
Underpayment of taxes, 65–66

Vacate, 163
Vendor/vendee, 173
Venue, 100
  change of, 100
Verdicts, 147
  directed, 147
  not reaching, 162
  returning, 163
Vested rights and interests, 173–74
Violations, 117–19
Void, 45
Voidable, 46
Voluntary, 177

Ward, 171
Warrant
  arrest, 153
  bench, 153
  defined, 135, 153
  of habitability, 85
  search, 153
Warranty, 85
White-collar crime, 183
Wills, 18, 54–60, 135
  defined, 55–56, 135
Witness(es), 129–30
  physical examination of, 145
Writ, 136
  of certiorari, 136
  of execution, 136
  of habeas corpus, 136
Wrongful-death statutes, 18

Zoning regulations, 79

ABOUT THE AUTHOR

Miriam Kurtzig Freedman, a former teacher, is a graduate of Barnard College and New York University School of Law. Currently a practicing attorney, she lives near Boston with her husband and children.